david Rowland

David Rowland
40/4 Chair

Erwin Rowland Laura Schenone

Contents

Foreword

David Rowland is among a unique group of groundbreaking modernists whose particular chair defines them in the history of design. This illustrious members' club includes Charles Eames and his 1956 Lounge Chair #670, Hans Wegner and his 1949 Round Chair JH501, and Ludwig Mies van der Rohe for his 1929 Barcelona Chair MR 90.

Similarly, the 40/4 Chair has defined Rowland's legacy. When it was introduced in 1964, it launched a whole new category of seating: compactly stackable moveable chairs. Its unique geometry and use of steel-rod frames with stamped-steel seats and backs facilitated the stackability of forty chairs within a height of only 4 ft (1.2 m). It broke other boundaries also. A stack of forty chairs could be rolled away on a single dolly by one person and stored in a very small space. The chairs could be ganged together in rows and one row stacked on another row or several rows. Plus it was designed ergonomically for comfortable long-term sitting, and its elegant and spare aesthetic allowed it to fit seamlessly into diverse settings. Six decades later, the 40/4 not only remains the standard for compactly stackable moveable chairs, but also endures as a unique and consequential commercial product. In 2010, I named the 40/4 Chair one of the top ten commercial interiors products of the prior fifty years, unsurpassed in its engineering sophistication and production.

As often is the case with innovation, once a need is filled, the solution seems as though it should have been self-evident all along. But at the time of the 40/4's creation, no one seemed to have realized the value of tackling the challenge of creating compactly stackable, portable seating. Rowland did. Through countless rounds of improvement and refinement over many years, he harnessed the rudimentary issues of chair design and transformed what could have been a mundane solution into a piece of enduring brilliance.

And yet, despite its huge impact, the 40/4's inventor has been far less well known than the usual suspects of iconic mid-century chair design listed earlier. This book changes that. It shines a light on David Rowland, the man behind the chair, his life, his design philosophy, his other work, and his winding path to success as an independent industrial designer who forged his own way without being part of a design firm. Drawing on his copious archives as well as first-hand stories, authors Erwin Rowland and Laura Schenone bring to light the influences, character, and thinking that made Rowland's success possible. These include his upbringing in California, where he was exposed to art and culture from birth; studying under László Moholy-Nagy of the Bauhaus as a teenager; being a bomber pilot in World War II before he was twenty; his education at Cranbrook Academy of Art, which encouraged unbridled imagination; and his work and experiences in New York with such great designers as Norman Bel Geddes, Maria Bergson, Florence Knoll, and R. Buckminster Fuller, all of whom forced him continuously to raise his expectations and the standards of his own work.

While David's inspirations and influencers set his high design standards, the real business world of professional industrial design was another matter. There he experienced many setbacks, including a disappointing meeting with the curator Edgar Kaufmann Jr., at the Museum of Modern Art in New York, a lack of interest from the designer George Nelson and the Herman Miller company, and the abrupt cancellation of a major licensing deal with Knoll Associates for no apparent reason. David's salvation was his faith and perseverance, which eventually led him to the manufacturer that ultimately catapulted the 40/4 Chair to success as the design icon it is today.

With a wealth of images from his life and work—including Rowland's first sketches of the 40/4 Chair, and its current iterations in a stunning range of settings—this book is an inspiring addition to the history of industrial design and invention.

I was once introduced to David Rowland; I only wish our paths would have crossed again. I am glad that, through this book, I get to know him and his extraordinary chair better—and that others will too.

Carl Gustav Magnusson
Industrial designer, inventor, design juror, and lecturer.

Introduction

How did the 40/4 Chair come into being? What makes it special? Why is it chosen to furnish beautiful architectural settings all over the globe? And, why has it endured as one of the most important designs of the twentieth century? This book answers these questions and many others, and places this remarkable chair in the context of the life and work of its designer.

The 40/4 Chair—which can be stacked forty high in just 4 ft (1.2 m)—was not a spontaneous invention. It was the creation of the industrial designer David Rowland, who conceived it and then developed it for almost a decade. Therefore, to understand the 40/4 Chair fully, one must understand the character, experiences, and thought processes of David Rowland.

David was committed to doing the most with the least and fitting things together in the smallest, most efficient space. This applied not only to stackable chairs but also to all his designs—and even to the cars we drove. For most of our marriage, David and I lived in an apartment building in New York City and parked our car on the street outside. He always wanted us to have a very small car because it was convenient for driving in the city and made it easier to find a parking space, but, whatever car we had, it always had a sunroof, because that greatly expanded the capacity. David often had steel rods and other materials sticking out through the sunroof. It was amazing how much he could fit into those small cars, often as many as three or four chairs, plus us. I would be convinced that they wouldn't fit, but he would turn the chairs upside down and around in such a way that they all went in.

Another important trait of David's was that he didn't readily accept it when he was told that something was impossible. He was always determined to think of a solution. He loved to think. In fact, thinking was one of his favorite things to do, usually thinking about how to solve problems. If he was waiting in the car while I was running errands, he was never impatient because he enjoyed using the time to think.

David didn't give up on the things he believed in. He worked on the 40/4 Chair for a long time before finding a manufacturer, never giving up on his idea. He just continued working to refine and improve it. When the chair was finally accepted, it became an immediate international success.

Because design, and life, don't happen in a vacuum, we have included in this book the context and experiences of David's life as they were instrumental to his

design philosophy and career. I also want to correct the misconception that David designed only one thing, the 40/4 Chair, because this is far from the truth. He designed many things throughout his career, including cars, lighting, and furniture, and although not everything he designed was produced, all pushed design boundaries in some way, as evidenced by the fact that he held thirty-seven U.S. utility patents for his work. This book includes highlights from David's entire body of work, as well as his commitment to solving the problems faced by people in their everyday lives. It also illustrates the prescience of his thinking, which we see in, for example, his flat-packed sofa, at a time when self-assembly was a new idea; a safer ashtray; a seating material that provided great comfort without bulk; ways of using shipping containers as housing; and concepts relating to solar energy and wind power.

There is an additional reason for this book, albeit a personal one. David Rowland and I were married for thirty-nine years, so I bring a unique perspective. I was his only wife, and we did not have children. David himself was an only child. I have inherited his story and all his archives of drawings, sketches, models, plans, photographs, letters, and files. If we are driven to understand what kind of life and influences make outstanding creative accomplishments possible, I feel obligated to put all this on record, filling in a piece of design history that would otherwise pass on with me. I believe that the stories of artists and creative people need to be told.

Erwin Rowland

The First Compactly Stackable Chair

" My goal was to create the most universal chair ever built with the least expenditure of materials and labor. "

One hot Sunday afternoon in the mid-1950s, the young industrial designer David Rowland was sitting at his drawing board in his small, rented room in New York City, "listening for ideas," when the thought came to him: Why don't you see how many chairs you can get into the smallest space? He began plotting and laying out the ideas as they came to him, producing, to his amazement, a design so slim and compact that forty chairs could be stacked in a height of only 4 ft (1.2 m). It was an unprecedented achievement that would pioneer an entirely new category of seating.

Rowland's design—later called the 40/4 ("forty in four") Chair—would ultimately win international awards, earn numerous patents, sell in the millions, and be named one of the most important interior product designs of the twentieth century. The chair would be featured in the permanent collections of major museums around the world and used in every conceivable type of environment, including educational settings, hospitality venues, public buildings, healthcare facilities, cultural sites, and places of worship. It would remain in continuous production for sixty years—and counting. Today, the 40/4 Chair is part of the built environment, widely viewed as a masterpiece and one of the most successful chairs of all time.

And yet, because Rowland was on his own, an independent designer without the backing of a firm or team, it took him nine years to find a manufacturer and bring his idea to fruition. The earliest sketch of the 40/4 is dated 1954, but it wasn't until 1963 that Rowland had his breakthrough and signed a successful licensing contract, and not until the following year that the chair finally made its public debut at the Museum of Modern Art, in New York City. Along the way, he knocked on the door of one company after the next, facing rejection, stumbling blocks, and indifference.

Many inventions have been born as the result of chance or happy accident, but nothing could be further from the truth for the 40/4, which came into the world because of the designer's imagination, originality, skill, and dedication over many years. In this way, the story of the 40/4 Chair is a story of a man whose faith and persistence would not let him give up, as much as it is the story of a revolutionary design. It is impossible to tell one without telling the other.

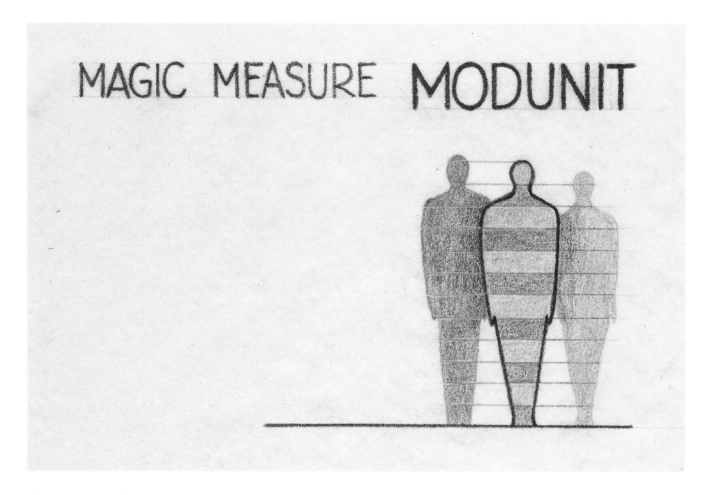

Developing the idea

When the inspiration for the 40/4 Chair came to him that summer day, Rowland was working hard to make his own path. He'd arrived in New York City only a couple of years earlier, fresh from Cranbrook Academy of Art, eager and optimistic, or, as he later described it, "with no cash and a few ideas." Chair design had intrigued him since he was a boy—he'd built his first one at age fourteen. Seating also held special personal importance for him because he had piloted B-17 bomber planes in World War II. During long missions, the seats in the planes gave him so much misery that he resolved to create comfortable seating if he made it out of the war alive.

Like countless designers before and after him, Rowland faced the extraordinary challenges inherent in chair design. A chair must stand up under proportionally many times greater stress than a bridge or building, but without the foundations in the ground to give it strength. As Ludwig Mies van der Rohe is frequently quoted, "The chair is a very difficult object. Everyone who has ever tried to make one knows that. There are endless possibilities and many problems—the chair has to be light, it has to be strong, it has to be comfortable. It is almost easier to build a skyscraper than a chair."

Rowland was adamant that most chairs failed because they were poorly designed, did not conform to the shape and needs of the human body, or created fatigue and pain. "It's easier to design 5,000 chairs that are different than to find five that really fulfill the two basic requirements of beauty and comfort," he said, describing a large percentage of public seats as "instruments of torture" because they were designed for looks first and comfort afterward.

Rowland developed
his own system for
measurement called
Maximum Ordering
Dimension (MOD).
His basic unit of
measure, the MOD,
was 5 and 5/8 inches
long and could be
used to calculate ideal
sizing for products;
for example, three
MODs for seating height,
five for tables,
and fourteen for the
length of beds. The
40/4 Chair is based
on the MOD system.

Rowland was committed to comfort, so he started with human anatomy rather than styling. With the help of his mother, Neva, he wrote to governments around the world, requesting data on body measurements. With this information, he created his own system for sizing products to fit the greatest number of people. He called it Maximum Order Dimensioning (MOD). Using MOD, he concluded that the ideal seat for the 40/4 would be 17 in (43 cm) from the ground and the same deep. He created slight contours in the chair seats and backs to enhance comfort and support. He also created "give," so the sitter could shift and move naturally, using a strong but flexible base of thin metal for both seat and back. The metal was covered with a special vinyl coating for a non-metallic feeling.

Although a few stackable chairs existed at the time, none were compactly stackable and portable to the extent of the 40/4. The extreme space-saving qualities of Rowland's chair set it apart from all others and introduced a new type of seating that could be set up and taken down quickly, then rolled on a dolly and stored in a remarkably small space. All kinds of environments—from huge venues to small gatherings—could be transformed with a minimum of time, effort, and storage.

Rowland worked on the design off and on for many years in a process of continuous refinement down to the smallest details. A slim frame, built with 7/16 in (1.1 cm) steel rod, emerged as key to the design. This narrow rod enabled the chair's compact stackability, while also giving it strength and stability. From there, Rowland kept experimenting with measurements, various angles, and contours to perfect the chair's overall comfort and function. This led to an increasing number of unique features. For example, he added a "ganging system" that allowed the chairs to be linked in a row that could be lifted, moved, and even stacked on another row without disconnecting. He attended to such small details as snap-on glides to protect floor surfaces. Later, he would say, "My goal was to create the most universal chair ever built with the least expenditure of materials and labor."

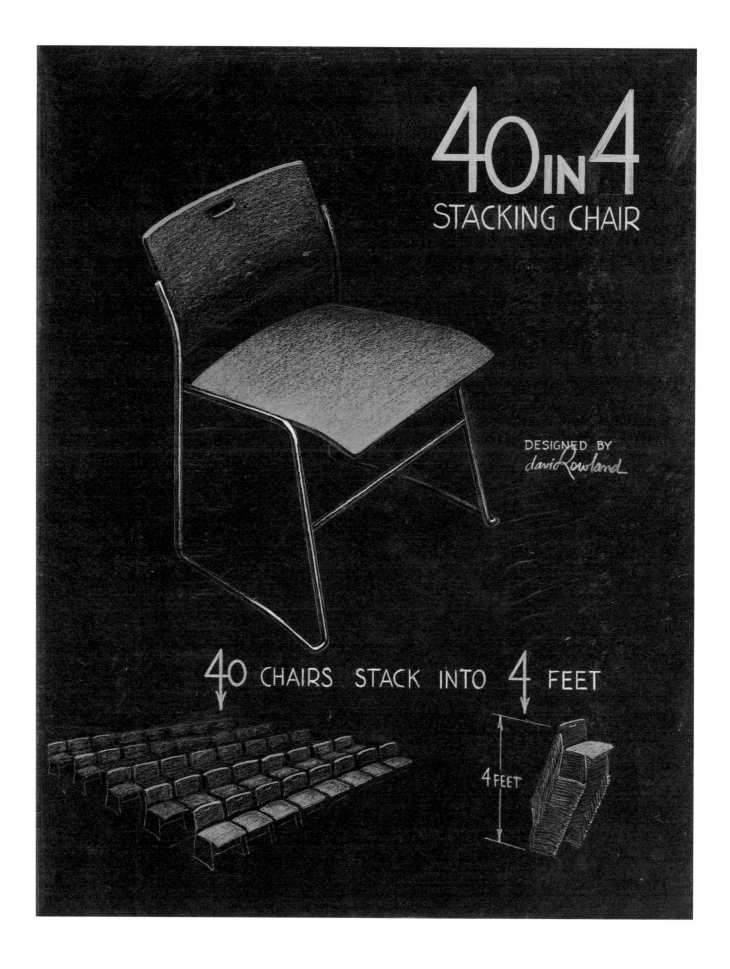

Early drawing for
Rowland's "40 in 4"
stackable chair.

There is no market for a stackable chair

Rowland sought expert advice on the best way to prototype, license, and manufacture the chair—daunting tasks to face alone. He decided to reach out to Edgar Kaufmann Jr., head of the department of architecture and design at the Museum of Modern Art (MoMA) in New York, as well as a longtime curator of its legendary Good Design program, which championed modern product design of the highest caliber. Kaufmann was highly influential in the American design scene. He also came from the prominent family that had founded the Kaufmann chain of department stores. As a young man he worked in the flagship store in Pittsburgh as a merchandising manager, specializing in modern furniture and fabrics. He was notable for having encouraged his father to commission the architect Frank Lloyd Wright to build Fallingwater (1937), the family's country home outside of Pittsburgh and one of the most extraordinary house designs in the United States.

Kaufmann agreed to see Rowland, and Rowland arrived, full of optimism, for the meeting. He walked through the doors of the museum believing that surely Kaufmann would see the value and marketability of his new chair. At this point, Rowland had only sketches of the design and two small-scale models to show. He hoped that Kaufmann might talk to him about prototyping and suggest companies to approach.

His hopes were dashed. After Rowland finished presenting his stackable chair idea, Kaufmann said that there was no market for a stackable chair in the United States. With that, the meeting was over, and Rowland left.

Walking down the street from the museum, he mulled over what had just happened, wondering if he should give up on the idea or continue despite this negative feedback. On the one hand, a leading expert had just told him his compactly stackable chair had no market value. Rowland did not take that lightly. But on the other hand, he believed in his design, his invention. Then another thought struck him, even more important. Rowland was a man of faith who believed that creative ideas come not from individuals, but from a greater source, the Divine Mind. For him, this meant God. He reasoned that if the idea for his new chair had come from God, then he couldn't give up. He'd have to fight for it.

By the time Rowland reached his apartment, he'd made his decision. He said to himself, "I'm going to do it anyway."

Stacking Chair

8 May 56

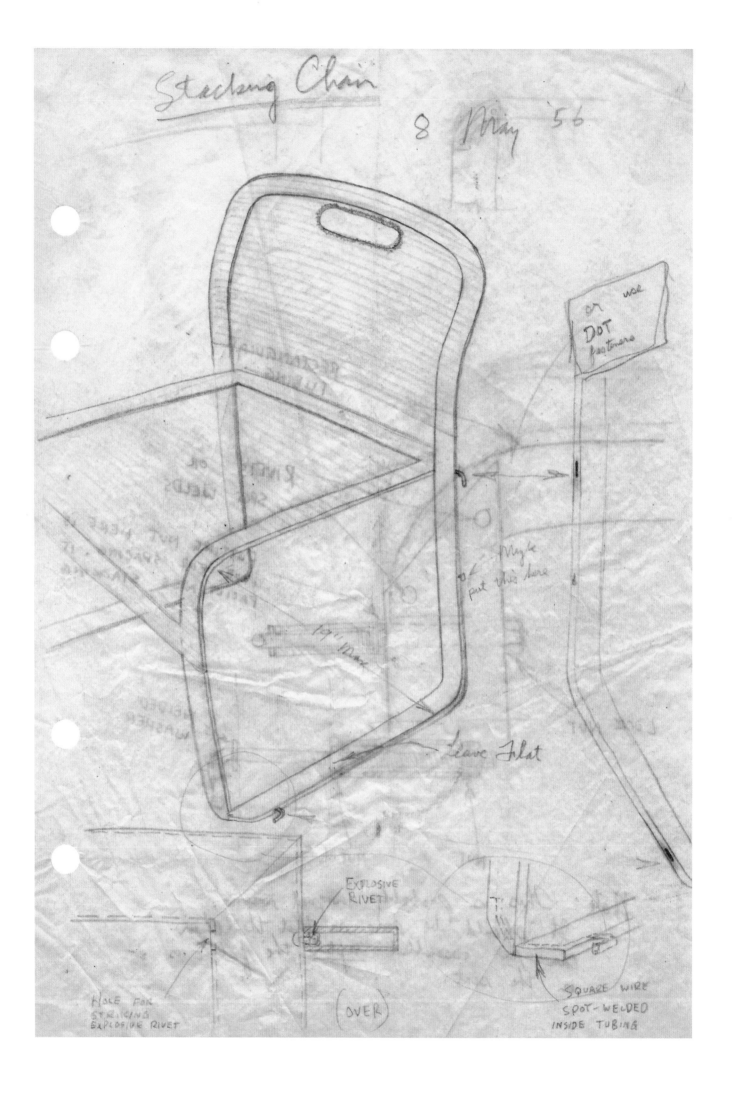

or use
DOT fasteners

Maybe
put this here

Leave Flat

EXPLOSIVE
RIVET

HOLE FOR
STACKING
EXPLOSIVE RIVET

(OVER)

SQUARE WIRE
SPOT-WELDED
INSIDE TUBING

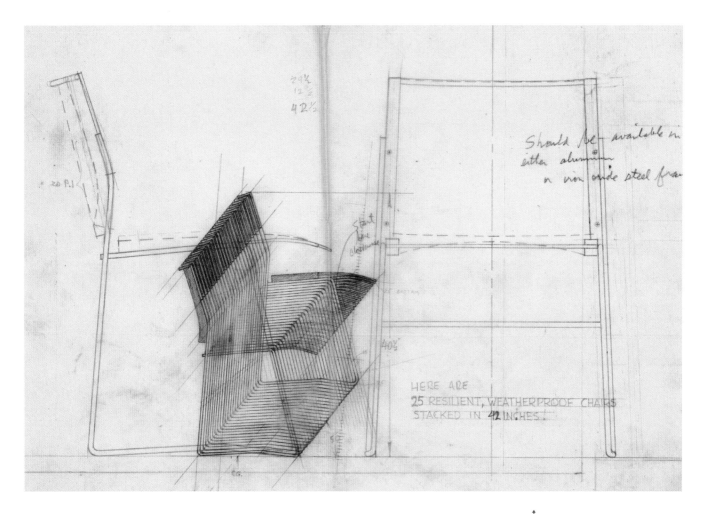

Within the drawing (handwritten notes):

29¾
12½
42½

Should be available in
either aluminum
or iron oxide steel frame

HERE ARE
25 RESILIENT, WEATHERPROOF CHAIRS
STACKED IN 42 INCHES

↑

Working out the idea:
an early rendering
of "25 resilient
waterproof chairs,"
stacked, 42 inches
tall, and available
in aluminum or steel.

←

Technical drawing
of the 40/4 Chair,
1956. Rowland refined
his "stacking chair"
design over many years,
experimenting with
various materials,
dimensions, curves,
and angles.

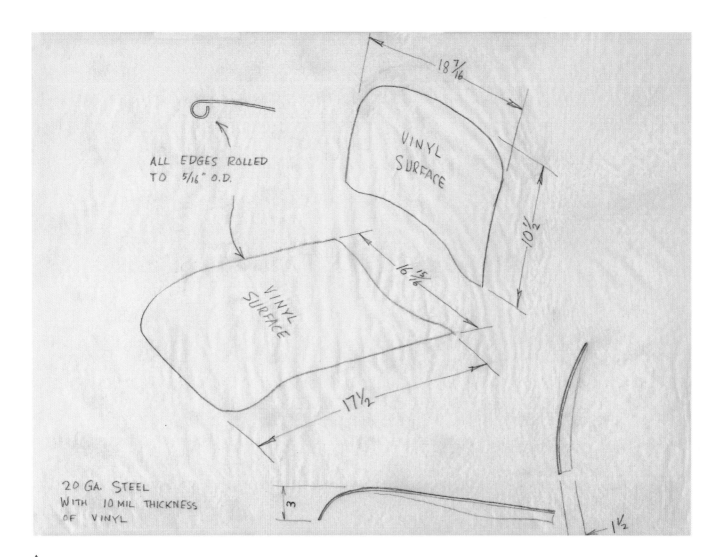

ALL EDGES ROLLED
TO 5/16" O.D.

VINYL SURFACE

VINYL SURFACE

18 7/16

10½

16 15/16

17½

3

1½

20 GA. STEEL
WITH 10 MIL THICKNESS
OF VINYL

↑
When he designed the
40/4 Chair, comfort was
one of Rowland's chief
aims. The seat and back
were cast in steel but
coated with a vinyl
surface, and the front
edge curved downward
so the sitter's knees
would be slightly
lower than the hips,
relieving stress.

→
The 40/4 Chair, 1964,
at the Museum of
Modern Art in New York
City, where it debuted
ten years after the
earliest known sketch.

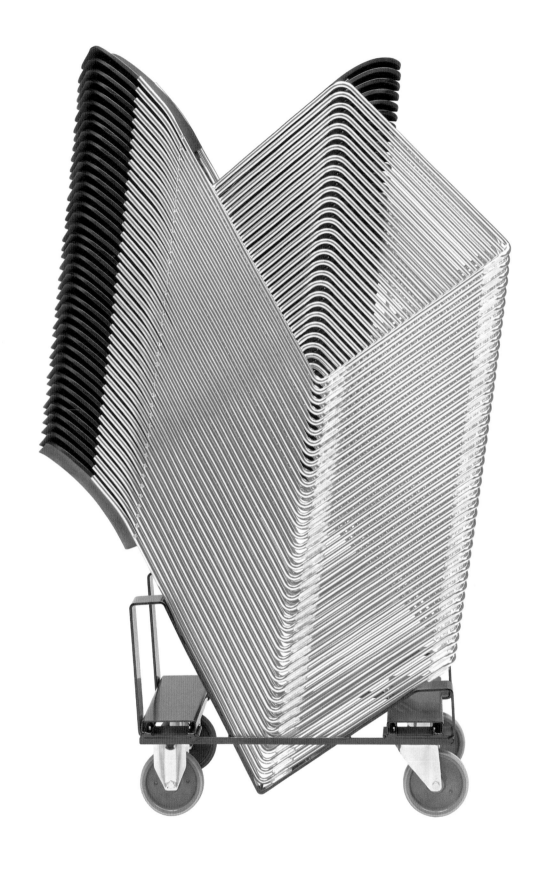

David Rowland: 40/4 Chair

↑
Rowland's patented
dolly was a key feature
of his invention.
The dolly allowed a
stack of forty chairs
to be easily rolled,
creating unprecedented
portability, flexibility,
and storage potential.

Overleaf:
The iconic St. Paul's,
Cathedral in London,
which installed 3,500
40/4 Chairs.

Foundations of
Great Design:
Early Influences and
Experiences

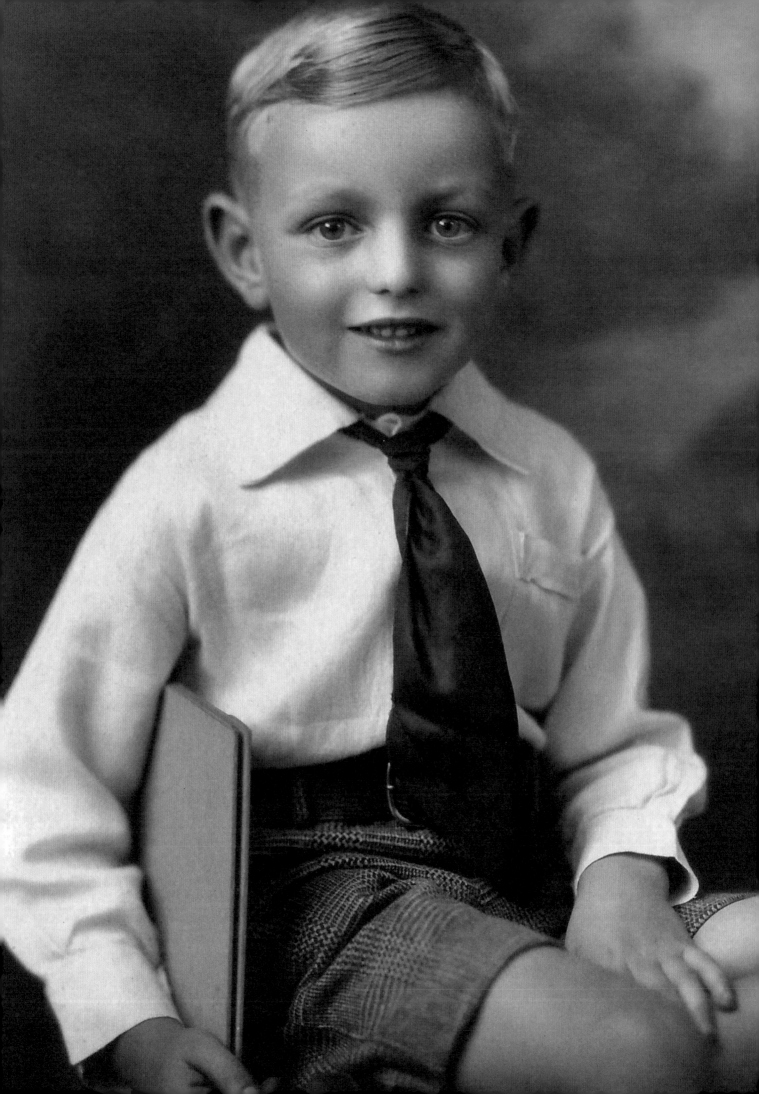

On February 12, 1924 in Hollywood, California, Earl Rowland, an Impressionist painter and member of the California Art Club, and his wife, Neva Rowland, a violinist, brought forth into the world their one and only child, David Lincoln Rowland. (The date was Abraham Lincoln's birthday, hence the middle name.) Years later, Earl would recall the moment, saying that David "became the center of our world."

Earl Rowland soon noticed his son's extraordinary talents. The boy loved to draw, and by six years old he could create three-dimensional renderings of peaches and pears that were far beyond his years. Perhaps it was not surprising, considering that Earl was himself an artist. He specialized in *plein-air* painting and often took his son with him to beautiful landscapes, giving the boy his own paints and brushes so they could work side by side. Earl also noticed that, in addition to his artistic talents, David showed an affinity for mechanical things, such as model airplanes and cars, and he liked to fix things or make them work better. In an apocryphal family story, Rowland was only five years old when he noticed his father had broken a drill and was about to throw it away. He asked if he could have the drill. Earl said yes. Rowland took it, repaired it, and returned it to his father, announcing it was fixed.

It was Earl who suggested to his son that he might like to become an industrial designer because the profession combined art and mechanical things. Rowland liked the sound of it and, when he was still a boy, decided that is what he'd do.

There are many ways to go about telling the life story of a great designer. We wonder what early experiences and influences set the stage for the decades of creativity and originality to come, what kind of formative moments or design philosophy made the difference and planted the seeds for great accomplishment.

In the case of David Rowland, many positive influences were at play from the very beginning, including inborn talent, unique exposure to fine art and culture, education with one of the greatest living design teachers, and the strength of religious faith. But it would be hard to overstate the positive influence of his parents. Neva and Earl Rowland were remarkable people in that they not only recognized their son's talent, but also poured extraordinary energy and support into helping him reach his goals. They had little money but were ready to shift their lives as needed to support their son's development. Earl, especially, took an active role in his son's success, guiding his personal and spiritual development, encouraging him to "aim for the top," and giving him constant encouragement. In this way, family love and the devotion of his parents were a direct, major influence on the career of David Rowland and, by extension, on his masterpiece, the 40/4 Chair.

Earl and Neva Rowland,
David's parents,
on their wedding day,
1919. Earl had joined
the army to serve in
World War I.

David Rowland: 40/4 Chair

A family history of adventurers

David Rowland's life story begins in Southern California during the 1920s—a time and place of boundless possibility and optimism. The region's gentle climate, growing motion picture business, oil, fertile land, and jobs had beckoned people by the thousands since the early part of the century. Both of Rowland's parents had been among the new arrivals seeking opportunity. Both had descended from adventurous families that traversed the continent, pursuing gold, dreams, and opportunities in the American West. Rowland's ancestors were industrious, boundary-pushing people and rugged individualists who showed remarkable resilience and willingness to strike out on their own—traits that were ultimately passed down through the family to him.

Rowland's father, Earl Rowland, had been born in Trinidad, Colorado, in 1890 to parents of Swiss, German, and English heritage who came West from Pennsylvania after the Civil War. Earl's father acquired some mines but lost them, and the family went into a state of economic struggle. Earl wanted a different life as an artist. By age nineteen, he left Colorado to attend the School of the Art Institute of Chicago. Along the way, he heard about the Church of Christ, Scientist and decided to pursue it. He became both an artist and a devout Christian Scientist.

Rowland's mother, Neva Chilberg, was born in 1892. Her mother, Millie, was descended from early French and English settlers in the Detroit area. Her parents went west to follow the Gold Rush and later established themselves in Washington Territory. Millie became a healer in Christian Science, which was then a new faith, established in 1879. Neva's father, Joseph Chilberg, was a colorful, and fearless man who would figure largely in Rowland's early life as a most fascinating grandfather. Joseph's parents had immigrated to America in the 1840s from Sweden. Joseph found his way to Washington State, where he and Millie met, married, and had Neva.

Neva was musical and studied violin from a young age. She had a free spirit and later remembered riding her horse and lying on her back looking up at the tall trees in the forest of Olympia. When she was about six years old, her father caught gold fever and raced to the Yukon and Alaska. He never found gold, but he opened the first grocery store in the boom town of Nome, Alaska, just across the Bering Sea from Russia. He sold to miners and traded with Indigenous People, who exchanged goods and artifacts for groceries. Chilberg became fascinated with Native Alaskan culture and opened a curio shop where he displayed these native objects and art. In 1906, Millie and Neva joined Chilberg in Nome, but after a couple of years they left for Chicago so that Neva could advance her study of the violin. To defray costs, they rented out a room in their apartment to Earl Rowland, a young art student whom they'd met in Christian Science circles. Earl and Neva became friends, but they parted ways when Earl left Chicago for California to be an artist and work in the movie business creating caption cards for silent films. They reunited when Neva also moved to the Los Angeles area, but their lives were interrupted when Earl joined the army to serve in World War I. Fortuitously, the day before he was to ship overseas, the war ended. In 1919, Neva and Earl got married. They were well suited to one another. Both were imaginative, energetic, and creative spirits. Both were Christian Scientists and artistic people.

→
Rowland's mother,
Neva Chilberg, was an
accomplished violinist.
Rowland recalled
hearing her practice
eight hours a day.

↓
Rowland descended from
a family of people who
struck out for the
unknown in the American
West. His grandfather,
Joseph Chilberg, was
a gold miner who opened
a grocery store in
Nome, Alaska, trading
with the miners and
Alaskan Natives.

David Rowland: 40/4 Chair

→
At the end of his life,
Rowland's grandfather
came to live with
the family. David
was a young child
and fascinated by his
collection of Native
Alaskan artifacts.

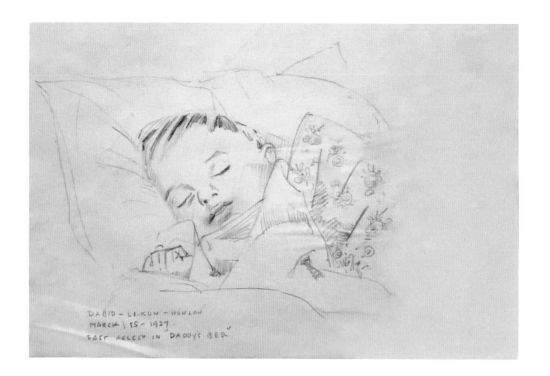

DABID - LI-KON - WOWLON
MARCH \ 15 - 1927.
FAST ASLEEP IN DADDY'S BED.

↑

Illustration of
Rowland, age three,
by his father, the fine
artist Earl Rowland.

→

From the time he was
a baby until age
thirteen, Rowland's
parents brought him
along to meetings of
the California Art
Club, held in Hollyhock
House, designed by
Frank Lloyd Wright.

The
CALIFORNIA
ART CLUB
BULLETIN

VOL. II   LOS ANGELES   AUGUST 1927   No. 8

THE LILY POND
CALIFORNIA ART CLUB—BARNSDALL PARK

A childhood surrounded by art and culture

Earl and Neva built a new home on Gardenside Lane in Los Angeles, and Earl developed an advertising business to support his family, in addition to sales of his paintings. As an artist, he received praise and attention for his Impressionist landscapes and other paintings. Neva played her violin and had a trio that performed at many types of venues and cultural events. She also had a radio program and conducted music programs for KHJ Los Angeles Times Station for more than twenty years. David Rowland spent his childhood surrounded by culture and art. His father was a member (and for some years treasurer) of the California Art Club (CAC), which included many of California's major Impressionist painters. The Rowlands attended monthly meetings, and, because they couldn't afford a babysitter, they regularly brought their son with them from the time he was a baby until he was age thirteen.

The location of these meetings was extraordinary: Hollyhock House, designed by Frank Lloyd Wright for the oil heiress Aline Barnsdall, who in 1927 welcomed the CAC to use her property. The main building was set on a 36 acre (14.5 hectare) plot, amid olive trees, with views of the Hollywood Hills. Every room had access to outdoor space. As he grew up, young Rowland had the opportunity regularly to wander the house and grounds, even the rooftop, and experience the wonder of its patios, pergola, natural wood paneling, stained-glass windows, furnishings, skylights, tall ceilings, grounds, and exquisite views. The environment must have seeped into his being—not only the house, but also the experience of being among artists who talked about art, made art, and exhibited their work. He absorbed his father's sensitivity to visual beauty and witnessed his mother's dedication to music. Both his parents were hard workers and dedicated to their crafts. He later recalled how his mother practiced her violin eight hours a day.

When David was still young, Neva's mother died, and her father came to live with the family for the last five years of his life. Joseph Chilberg had a great impact on his grandson, who was fascinated by his grandfather's collection of Native Alaskan artifacts. Rowland had the opportunity to handle, study, and think about them. His grandfather let him help arrange small items on display boards. Rowland was deeply impressed by native tools, such as an *adz*, a primitive cutting tool, which he later wrote about in graduate school, extolling the simplicity of its form designed to achieve function. It was a theme that he would carry through his life as a designer.

The Great Depression and its life-changing impact

The stock market crash of 1929 and the subsequent Great Depression created deep pain in the Rowland family. Earl, working harder and harder to make a living, had a nervous breakdown. Neva stepped up to help the family income by taking on more work with her trio at wedding receptions, parties for wealthy Southern Californians, and other events.

A door finally opened when the University of Redlands invited Earl to teach a summer course on art. This led to speaking engagements at women's clubs around the state, and additional opportunities to teach. His reputation grew, and he was invited to be the director of the Haggin Museum and Pioneer Galleries in Stockton, California (now the Haggin Museum). He accepted, and the family relocated 300 miles (482 km) north of Los Angeles to Stockton, where he worked tirelessly for the next twenty-six years. The job stabilized the family during the Depression, and, over the decades, the museum created transformational experiences, connections, and remarkable opportunities for the young Rowland.

The Haggin was a significant art and history museum that held the largest collection of works in the area by the noted California landscape artist Albert Bierstadt, paintings by Hudson River School painters, such as Thomas Moran and George Inness, and dozens of paintings by renowned European artists. The museum also had extensive historical galleries featuring Native Californians, the Gold Rush, agriculture in the San Joaquin Valley, machinery, tools, and California history. Just walking into the Haggin offered Rowland an explosion of imagination and inspiration. He was fascinated by it all, and, as a result, he developed a lifelong passion for museums and art. Stockton itself also offered new opportunities for Rowland. It was a small but ethnically diverse city that exposed him to new people and cultures he'd never known.

Earl worked to expand the museum's exhibits and holdings. One of his biggest contributions was to build the Haggin's landmark collection of works by the famous illustrator J. C. Leyendecker, a prolific painter and illustrator for *Collier's*, the *Saturday Evening Post*, and many famous American brands. Finding original Leyendecker paintings and prints became a passion for Earl, who enlisted David as his lookout agent when he later moved to New York. Earl also developed public educational programming, including a radio show about the museum, and brought renowned speakers to the Haggin, which ultimately created connections for Rowland. One of these was the architect, industrial designer, inventor, and futurist R. Buckminster (Bucky) Fuller, who later became David's mentor and friend.

Coming of age: A life-changing course with László Moholy-Nagy

Rowland's parents dedicated themselves to supporting their son's education and success. During a particular moment in high school when Rowland found French and algebra challenging, Neva, who had not graduated high school herself, learned both subjects so that she could help him with his homework. Outside of school, Rowland was always building and designing things. By the time he was fourteen he had built his first chair (a young effort to imitate the straight-back dining chairs he'd seen at Hollyhock House, designed by Wright), and he also built his desk and a lamp. He took a drafting course and won design awards, and he was passionate about cars (both drawing and driving them). When he was sixteen, he entered the California Ford Good Drivers League contest, which promoted safe driving habits among high-school students. He won third place out of 8,000 students. After school, he earned money selling books door to door, took a job at a cannery, and worked in a car act at the San Joaquin County Fair.

Everything changed in 1940, when a flyer crossed Earl's desk at the museum announcing that László Moholy-Nagy, the renowned Hungarian-born modern artist and Bauhaus teacher, would be offering a summer course at Mills College in Oakland. Earl understood it as a once-in-a-lifetime opportunity for his son and decided to seize it.

Obstacles had to be overcome. For one thing, Oakland was 55 miles (88 km) from Stockton, but, even more importantly, the course was for college students and Rowland was only a sophomore in high school. Nonetheless, understanding the importance of the course, Earl arranged for Rowland to meet with Moholy (as he was called) and requested a special waiver for Rowland's age. Moholy agreed, and Rowland enrolled in the eight-week course. Earl arranged for his vacation time from the museum to coincide, and when summer came, Earl and Neva put their belongings into storage and rented a place in Oakland so that Rowland could attend.

Moholy had taught at the Bauhaus School, the avant-garde German art school that was famous for its philosophy of unifying individual artistic vision with the principles of mass production and an emphasis on function. He was a strong advocate of the integration of technology and industry into the arts. When Adolf Hitler closed the school down in 1933 because of its modernist ideas and emphasis on individual expression, its faculty members scattered, and many fled the country. Moholy eventually wound up in the United States, where he helped to found the School of Design in Chicago (which continues today as a part of the Illinois Institute of Technology). His mission was to spread the Bauhaus philosophy and teaching methods to the United States. In this way David Rowland's life intersected not just with a great teacher but also with a fight for design as a force for good in the world at a critical moment in history. It was an awakening.

Today, the term "Bauhaus" is often understood as shorthand for a streamlined style of design, a certain look of twentieth-century modernism. But the movement's ambitions were far greater. The school was founded in Weimar, Germany, in 1919 by the architect Walter Gropius, who wanted to combine crafts and fine arts. Gropius and other Bauhaus teachers saw the threat of dehumanization in the rapid rise of industrialism. They advocated for human creativity and imagination and wanted to educate artists across creative disciplines to work with industry to create a better world that would meet human needs.

↓

David and his father,
Earl Rowland, who saw
his son's talents early
on and suggested he
might like to become an
industrial designer.

↘

László Moholy-Nagy and
his wife Sybil at a
birthday celebration
for Moholy, held during
the summer session
he conducted at Mills
College, 1940. Sixteen-
year-old Rowland is
in the background,
far right.

David Rowland: 40/4 Chair

According to the critic Patrick Sisson, "Moholy didn't focus on creating physical products; he focused on a philosophy, a way of thinking and approaching design problems. He envisioned a school that would educate the contemporary creator as an 'integrator, the new designer able to re-evaluate human needs warped by machine civilization'. He wanted to help men and women become artists and designers who realized their creative potential." Moholy believed that everyone is talented and taught his students an attitude of freedom and exploration, rather than adherence to fixed rules or fads, encouraging them to go beyond conventional boundaries of design and bring new inventions into the world. He also wanted his students to develop a "comprehensive knowledge of materials, tools, and function," which he believed was essential to being a designer in the new world of mass production. He evangelized that "the mass production of goods and modern architecture needed not only engineers but also artists with fresh mentality and exact information about old and new materials." David Rowland embraced this aim.

In the summer session, Moholy taught the students to explore the use of new and old materials. Rowland experimented with tools, machines, wood, metal, paper, plastic, wire, and lighting. Moholy also taught the foundations of three-dimensional design and a consciousness of volume and space. The students made photograms, a type of camera-less photography that places an object directly on sensitized paper and exposes it to light. This form, which challenges the viewer to see photography in a new way, was one of Moholy's signature interests. In one session, Moholy held up one of Rowland's photograms before the class and said with a big smile, "Zat's vanderful," in his heavy accent. It was an encouraging moment for the sixteen-year-old. Decades later, Rowland wrote, "I look back so many times to when a devoted teacher said some encouraging words to me. How much of success is because someone who cared made an effort at encouragement."

Moholy's teaching had a profound impact on Rowland. In that single summer, he acquired not only skills and techniques but also a way of thinking that guided his entire career, including the invention of the 40/4 Chair. He often referred to that summer as the best of his life.

David Rowland: 40/4 Chair

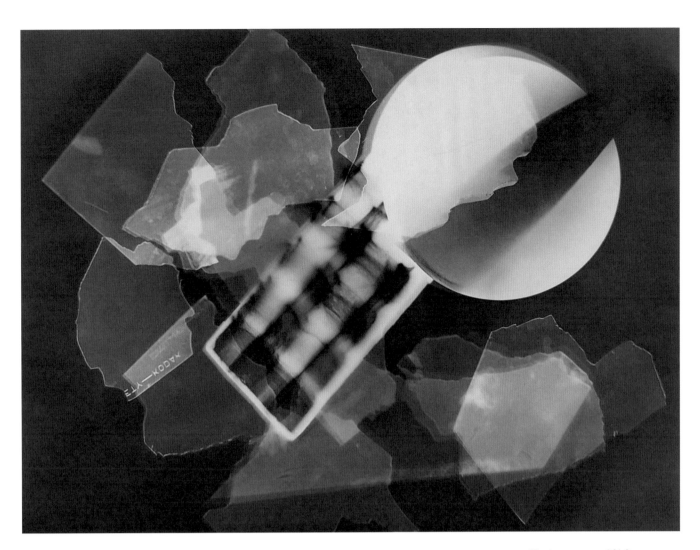

Photograms, 1940.
At age sixteen, Rowland
took a summer course
in basic Bauhaus design
with renowned artist
and teacher László
Moholy-Nagy. Using
Moholy's experimental
technique, he created
these images without
a camera by placing
ordinary objects on
photographic paper and
exposing them to light.

Rowland produced these
tempera paintings
for his course with
Moholy-Nagy, 1940.
The Bauhaus curriculum
featured intense study
of simple shapes and
primary colors.

David Rowland: 40/4 Chair

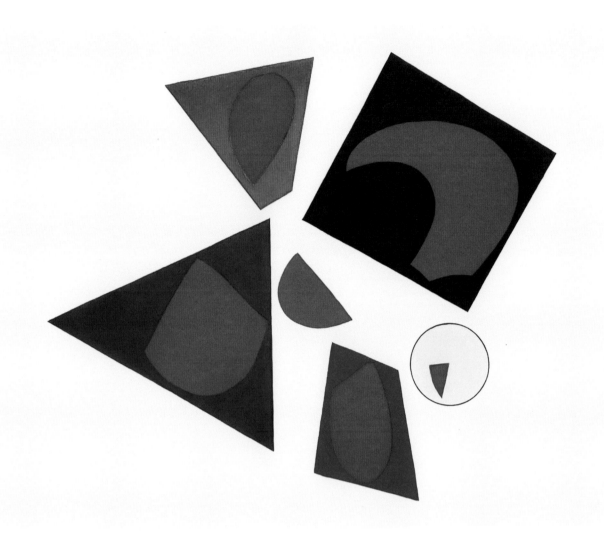

↑
Place setting for
Bauhaus course,
Rowland, 1940.
A study in contours,
shadow, and light.

→
Rowland's sketch
for a mobile,
coursework, 1940.

David Rowland: 40/4 Chair

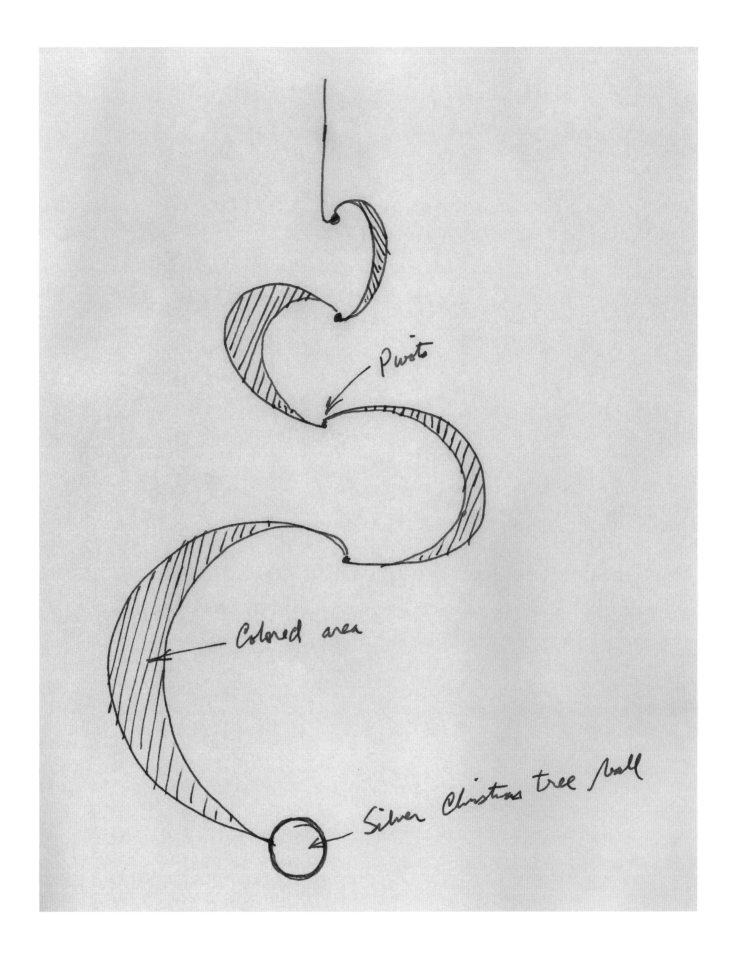

Pivot

Colored area

Silver Christmas tree ball

In the pilot's seat: World War II

As Rowland graduated from Stockton High School in 1942, World War II was on, and he got a job with Rheem Manufacturing in Stockton as a detail draftsman, drawing engineer's plans for bomb-making machinery and practice bombs. In the evenings he took courses in literature and marine architecture at the University of the Pacific.

In January 1943, just before his nineteenth birthday, Rowland volunteered for the U.S. Army Air Corps with the goal of being a pilot. He aspired to fly the P-38, a single-seat bomber, but the training was very difficult for him. He struggled at the beginning, and, after failing initial tests, he was uncertain whether he would pass over-all. In August 1943, he wrote his parents, sharing his earnest hope to do his best, as well as his fears and his faith. He cites a "comforting sentence" from Mary Baker Eddy, founder of the Church of Christ, Scientist.

> I think it's the thing for everyone to seek the most important job he can do according to his resources. It didn't seem the thing for me to do to stay at a drafting table and I can see now that it was because I wasn't using enough of my physical resources. Flying a P-38 (if I get that far) will take nearly all my physical and mental resources. God doesn't want us to be slackers in the race. The one comforting sentence that has been with me thru thick and thin … is "Whatever is your duty to do you can do without harm to yourself." Right now, I feel a little scared to fly a P-38. It is the utmost in drawing on one's resources, travelling at over 500 and being capable of taking more "G's" (a G is the force of gravity, 32.3 ft per second acceleration) than the average pilot can stand. The reason I am choosing it as a goal is that it is the top and I know you want me to have the "top" as my goal or I wouldn't be expressing the perfect man. However, if these physical or mental resources don't permit, there will be just as important a job farther down the line. I don't, and you don't want me to be, a slacker in the race. According to his resources my dad was not a slacker when he was in the army.

Training lasted two years, and during that time Rowland went to fifteen military bases in the United States, undertaking difficult and at times terrifying training, including one instance in California when his engine failed, and he had to make an emergency landing. In a telling moment, he decided not to let his anxiety show to his instructor and put a smile on his face. Shortly afterward, Earl and Neva visited their son at the base, and the instructor told them, "You've got quite a son. We were in deathly circumstance where we were bound to have serious injury, if not be killed, because of the wheels getting trapped in the mud, and your son has a broad grin on his face."

Rowland passed his pilot training and was assigned an even bigger aircraft than the P-38: the B-17 bomber, known as the Flying Fortress, a four-engine machine destined for strategic bombing campaigns of World War II. In January 1945, he shipped out overseas on the RMS Aquitania, encountering a freak storm with 70 ft (21 m) waves breaking over the bow and the constant threat of torpedo attack from German submarines, which had sunk the ship ahead of theirs just the day before. After landing in Scotland, he went on to Rougham Air Base near the town of Bury St. Edmunds in East Anglia. He was the youngest pilot there.

Rowland and his crew flew twenty-four missions, usually starting at three or four in the morning and lasting up to twelve or thirteen hours. They flew from England to their targets in Germany, dropped bombs, and headed back to England, while flying through flak and German artillery, facing an ever-present threat of death, and in some

Rowland piloted the B-17 Bomber during World War II. On long missions from England to Germany, the seats proved unbearable. He resolved he would design comfortable seating if he survived the war.

cases witnessing the planes of their peers being shot down around them. Before each mission Rowland read a passage of scripture to his crew over the intercom. Because one of his crew members was Jewish, he chose from the Old Testament. The B-17 was built for ten people, and Rowland's primary concern was always for the safety of his crew. The idea of such responsibility resting on the shoulders of a twenty-one-year-old is mind-boggling. He was taken aback when one of his crew, twenty-eight years old, called him "boss."

During these long missions, the bucket seats in the plane were painfully uncomfortable. Rowland vowed that if he survived the war, he would do something about it. It was a vow he would keep. The missions being so long, he had a lot of time to study what was wrong. The experience awakened his desire to create comfortable seating. This concern for comfort would become a theme that ran through his entire career and appeared in all the chairs he ever designed.

Letters from home provided a lifeline of encouragement that helped Rowland to get through the war. His father wrote almost every day, sending his son spiritual guidance, love, and advice, and generally keeping his spirits up. Decades later, Rowland often said he didn't know if he could have done what he did without those letters. In his own correspondence home, he certainly released some of the awful things he'd witnessed. In one letter, he described being in London, returning to his hotel one evening, when "the sky lighted up with an orange glow and then there was a huge explosion. It was a V-bomb and landed just five blocks away, breaking windows for blocks." This V-2 rocket took down a block of buildings and all the people who had been in those buildings and on the streets. It missed the British Museum by about three streets. (When Rowland visited London many years after the war, he saw that block still empty and was haunted by the memory.)

The letters between Rowland and his parents also reveal the depth of religious faith and prayer in the family. Earl frequently reminded his son of God's love, and of his own expectations for Rowland's strong moral character. In one particular letter, Earl quoted a line from the 23rd Psalm, "Thou preparest a table before me in the presence of mine enemies," and told Rowland, "On your flying missions, remember that the Lord, your Shepherd, will prepare a landing field for you right in the presence of your enemies, if you need one."

Months later, when Rowland was over enemy territory, two of his four engines were put out of commission, and he fell behind his group. After three hours alone in enemy skies and with little fuel left, he desperately needed to land. His predicament was compounded by dense cloud cover all the way to the horizon. He was losing altitude and bailing out seemed to be the only alternative for him and his crew. Then he remembered his father's words. He kept praying and thinking about it, and a few minutes later he was astounded to see an opening in the clouds revealing the crisscross pattern of an airfield. He came in and made a safe landing. He and his crew were in friendly territory in northern France.

On leave from duty during the war, Rowland took every opportunity to go to London and visit cultural sites and meet with people in the design world.

David Rowland: 40/4 Chair

Art, design, and culture—even during war

In addition to religious faith, Rowland turned to his own creativity and love of art and design to help him survive the war. After that harrowing landing in France, he wrote home that his crew had landed in the town of Merville, where they spent the night in a school. He noted that there were Bauhaus lights hanging from the ceiling—recognizing them from a book he'd seen. Rowland was always thinking about modern design and art. When he had a break, he would take a bike out to the beautiful countryside around his base and find peace in sketching on the grounds of a bombed-out manor house. He would also go into a nearby chapel to draw the pews, particularly the oak ends, each one a different design.

Rowland tried to make the most of his leaves to experience the culture and art of London, even as it was under siege. He wanted to keep his eyes open to see the world, which meant seeing not only the destruction, but also the beauty. His father constantly recommended people for him to meet and places for him to visit when he was in London. Rowland sought out these experiences and others, including visits to the Victoria and Albert Museum, the National Gallery, and the British Museum, even though most collections were removed for safekeeping. He wrote home describing how he toured St. Paul's Cathedral "from crypt to dome," where he got a good view of London. On another pass from duty, he met Princess Elizabeth and Queen Elizabeth, when they visited his officers' club. When duty took him on a brief visit to Marrakesh, Morocco, he marveled at the palaces, gardens, and mosques, captivated by the Islamic architecture and the dazzling colors. There were also modern buildings in Marrakesh. While he was there, Rowland saw a man standing on the balcony of a modern apartment building and called up to him, asking to see his apartment. Remarkably, the man came running down and welcomed Rowland up to give him a look.

Rowland's career aspirations remained foremost in his mind. In one letter, he told his parents of visiting the book designer Sir Francis Meynell, who went before Parliament to obtain the Charter for the Design Council in Britain. Rowland talked with him about what it took to be an industrial designer in Britain. In a used bookshop, when he spotted a 1923 edition of *Staatliches Bauhaus in Weimar 1919–1923* (the book that introduced the Bauhaus to the world) he snatched it up for the equivalent of six dollars. It was a prize. A few minutes later he visited an avant-garde publisher who offered him $200 for it, but Rowland declined. The book reminded him of Moholy and the Bauhaus course he'd taken. He wouldn't part with it for anything.

Rowland also corresponded with Moholy during his time at war. Moholy, who had spent time in England, wrote back with recommendations for what he might do with his free time. "My dear Rowland. I was thrilled with your letter for many reasons, mainly, that in spite of your martial job you have time and interest to care for cultural matters in which, as you know, we so much believe." He referred Rowland to many successful people he knew in the art and design world in Europe: "You may see Henry Moore, the sculptor, Herbert Read, the art critic, and Kurt Schwitters, the German Dadaist who lives in London. Perhaps in the meantime Ben Nicholson, Barbara Hepworth, and [Naum] Gabo have returned to London. Give them my heartiest greetings when you see them." (Rowland indeed met many of them, including Read.) Moholy also sent workshop materials that might inspire Rowland and reported that the Bauhaus design school he was building in Chicago was coming along well. He suggested that Rowland spread the word to soldiers who might be interested in attending after the war. A year later, Moholy died of leukemia. His mentorship was irreplaceable for Rowland.

INSTITUTE of DESIGN

June 30, 1945

1st Lt. David L. Rowland, O-2015212
333rd Sq., 94th Bomb Group
A.P.O. 559, c/o Postmaster
New York, New York

My dear Rowland:

I was thrilled with your letter for many reasons, mainly, that in spite
of your martial job you have time and interest to care for cultural
matters in which, as you know, we so much believe.

In the last few years all my friends left Germany except perhaps one
or two whom, if the non-fraternization order will be lifted, you may
see. One is Dr. Eric Schott, Jena, the director of the Schott Works,
whose sister worked with Zeiss. The other is Adolph Behne, an art
critic who was a splendid writer on modern art and architecture. He
lived in Berlin.

In England you may see Henry Moore, the sculptor, Herbert Read, the
art critic, and Kurt Schwitters, the German Dadist who lived in London.
Perhaps in the meantime Ben Nicholson, Barbara Hepworth, and Gabo have
returned to London. Give them my heartiest greetings when you see them.

Our school is developing nicely. We moved to a new and more formidable
location, and our summer semester starts next week.

I am enclosing a reprint on our photography workshop and one on design
potentialities, together with our summer term folder.

I think you could do a good envoy job for the Institute among your
colleagues in the armed forces, as we are acknowledged by the Veterans
Administration for the training of veterans.

With kind regards.

Very sincerely yours,

L. Moholy-Nagy

➤ **new address:**

LMN:mgk

1609 North State Street, Chicago 10, Illinois ● Telephone DELaware 4688-4690

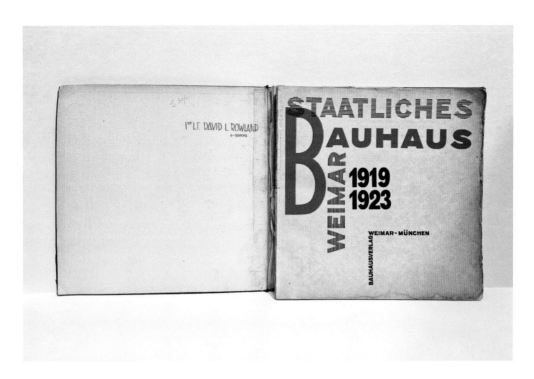

After the war was over in Europe, Rowland and his crew were assigned to stay on in England in case they were needed to go to Japan, where the fighting continued. In the meantime, they were required to keep up their flying time, and to do so they could fly anywhere within a certain range of their base. Rowland toured the cathedrals and famous landmarks of Europe by air in his B-17 with a small crew, seeing the places he had before seen only in books. He also was given assignments to fly personnel and supplies into Germany. He made these trips during the days immediately following surrender, when smoke was still billowing over the cities. On one such mission Rowland took the opportunity to fly over Nuremberg Stadium. Early in his pilot training, he had watched *Triumph of the Will*, the Nazi propaganda movie made by Hitler and the German film director and photographer Leni Riefenstahl, which featured the Nuremberg Congress and showed the stadium filled with swastikas and hundreds of thousands of troops saluting the Führer. It was a fearful picture that Rowland had not been able to get out of his mind. Now, as he looked down and saw American soldiers playing baseball in that same stadium, he felt the fear finally fade away.

Rowland returned home in September 1945, having achieved the rank of first lieutenant. He was only twenty-two when it was all over, and keen to get back to his life and resume his path to becoming an industrial designer.

Formal education: Principia College, University of Southern California, and Cranbrook Academy of Art

Newly home after the war, Rowland was eager to begin his education and professional training in design. He was accepted to Principia College, which he entered in January 1946. Situated on the bluffs of the Mississippi River in Elsa, Illinois, Principia was (and still is) a small liberal arts college for Christian Scientists. The 2,500-acre (1,012-hectare) campus featured the world's largest collection of buildings designed by the renowned architect Bernard Maybeck. It was an idyllic place. And although it was not the modern architecture that most interested Rowland, the campus was yet another environment of natural beauty and great architecture that influenced his life. He later said, "War was hell. Principia was heaven." It was a time and place for healing after the war.

The school did not offer industrial design, so Rowland majored in physics and minored in art, an ideal combination for his future work as an industrial designer. Art was easy for him. Although he found physics difficult, he liked it and knew it would be useful to his career. In 1949, he returned to California with a bachelor's degree and planned to go to graduate school the following fall, to study design. While he waited for space to open for him (schools were jammed with veterans returning from war), he went to Los Angeles, where he took valuable postgraduate courses at the University of Southern California (USC). He studied color theory and rendering (although his rendering instructor noted that Rowland's skills were so strong that he didn't need instruction). He'd always loved drawing. To make money on the side, he pumped gas and worked as a carpenter's helper building new homes. Mass-produced affordable housing was a lifelong interest for Rowland. During his time in Los Angeles, Charles and Ray Eames were experimenting with reasonably priced modern homes and building one for themselves, Case Study #8, in nearby Pacific Palisades. Rowland went over to observe and photograph the house being built.

At Principia College, with classmates, Rowland is at the far right with his hand in his pocket.

Rowland was gifted in
illustration. Here, a
study in perspective
done at USC (the
University of Southern
California), 1949.

The following January 1950, Rowland began a master's degree at Cranbrook Academy of Art in Bloomfield Hills, Michigan, one of the great design schools in the United States and a hotbed of American modernism and Bauhaus ideas. It was also a breeding ground for the best modern designers and chair-makers of the twentieth century, including Charles and Ray Eames, Harry Bertoia, Eero Saarinen, and Florence Knoll. In addition to its legacy of greatness, the campus had been designed by the renowned Finnish architect Eliel Saarinen (father of Eero), who had spent twenty-five years developing the buildings. Rowland described the campus as "one of the most beautiful manmade environments in the whole of the United States." His tuition was paid for by the GI Bill.

The educational environment was inspiring and thrilling. Cranbrook's inter-disciplinary curriculum favored nonconformist, original thinking. Students were encouraged to ask their own burning questions and answer these questions with experimentation and imagination. They were given the freedom to explore. This theme of independence and limitless thinking resonated with what was already inside of Rowland, and brought out the best in him. There were no grades, although at the end of the year, students learned if they'd passed or failed. Any student could visit any professor. Rowland often met with Carl Milles, the renowned Swedish sculptor, who was in residence at the time. Milles had created the Orpheus Fountain, a pool surrounded by sculptures of nymphs carrying poetry and art—a landmark sculpture on campus.

Cranbrook's spirit of holistic design fueled Rowland's creativity and talent. He learned how to use new materials and tools, particularly in metalsmithing and wood-working workshops, and explored unexpected ways of using them.

Molded veneer chairs, 1949, which Rowland built at his home after college and before he entered graduate school. The elegant and experimental Ribbon Chair was constructed of molded veneer.

A variation built on a tubular steel cantilever frame for flexibility.

David Rowland: 40/4 Chair

Illustrations of cars,
Rowland's coursework,
USC, 1949. From the
time he was a teenager,
Rowland loved cars.
Early on, he considered
a career in auto design.

↑
Rowland's architectural
drawing, 1949, reveals
his lifelong interest
in interior and
exterior architectural
design and his focus
on seating.

→
A study in negative
space featuring
contrasting warm and
cool colors, drawn
line, and painted
shapes by Rowland at
USC, 1949.

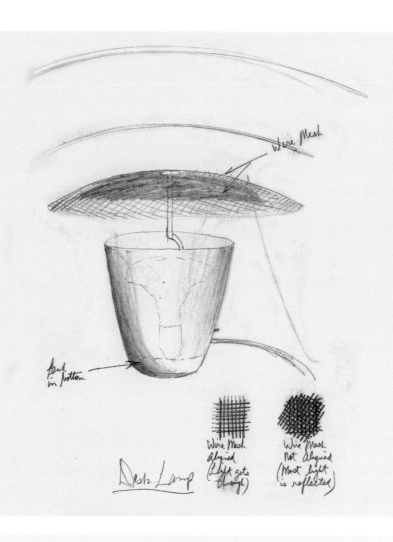

Wire Mesh

Seal
in bottom

Wire Mesh
Aligned
(Light gets
through)

Wire Mesh
Not Aligned
(Most light
is reflected)

Desk Lamp

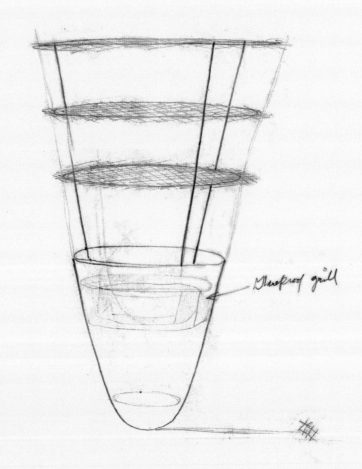

Glareproof grill

Drawing for a desk lamp (top) and a floor lamp (bottom), designed by Rowland at Cranbrook, 1951. A series of mesh screens diffuse and soften the light.

Floor lamp featuring a reflecting dome, designed and prototyped by Rowland at Cranbrook, 1951. It was weighted to give it stability.

David Rowland: 40/4 Chair

← Magic Carpet Chair, designed at Cranbrook. Rowland's first significant chair reveals his emerging lifelong interest in comfort without bulk. The seat and back were made of flexible steel wires woven with wool yarn.

↘ Zoltan Sepeshy (far right), longtime president of Cranbrook Academy of Art, in a studio with students.

First chairs

At Cranbrook, Rowland designed his first significant chair and named it the Magic Carpet Chair. His goal was to create a seat as comfortable as an upholstered chair—but without padding. He made the seat and back out of flexible steel wires, covered with vinyl tubing, then woven with red wool yarn made by his classmate Jack Lenor Larsen (later a famous textile designer). The seat could be adapted for use in cars, buses, and airplanes. The Korean War was on, and Rowland wanted to be true to his promise to create better seating in warplanes. That meant his Magic Carpet Chair had to be not only comfortable but also bulletproof, to protect pilots and passengers from enemy fire that might come from underneath them. His unique seating material achieved this purpose. To prove it, Rowland borrowed a forty-five caliber pistol from a school guard, set up his chair seat on an embankment, and fired away. The bullet flattened and didn't penetrate.

Sven Steen—a woodwork professor, and former cabinetmaker for Frank Lloyd Wright—used to come into Rowland's cubicle, smoking a pipe, and ask what he was working on. Rowland described the chair he was building and what he wanted to do. He later recalled what Steen told him: that if he succeeded, it would be the best thing that had happened at Cranbrook since Eames. This encouraged Rowland to work hard and do it right. When Steen came back for another visit, after Rowland had built the chair, he looked it over, sat on it, and bounced around a bit. "Better than Eames," he said and left.

Rowland continued to experiment with new seating materials and design. His next chair was the Spider Chair, which had a woven seat and back, like the Magic Carpet Chair, but also had armrests and a unique torsion-bar suspension base.

Rowland's Spider
Chair, 1951, featuring
a unique torsion bar
suspension frame
with a resilient woven
seat and back similar
to that of his Magic
Carpet Chair.

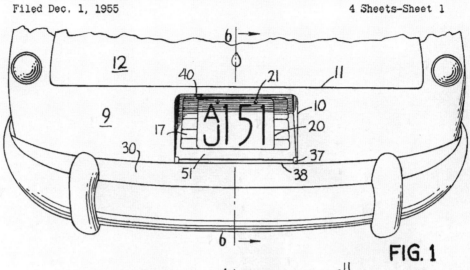

FIG. 1

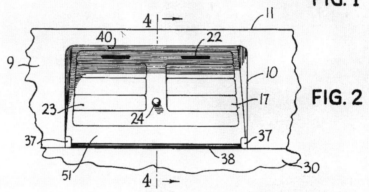

FIG. 2

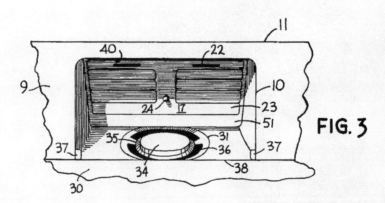

FIG. 3

INVENTOR.
DAVID L. ROWLAND
BY
ATTORNEY

Rowland's patent
drawings for a gas
cap located under the
car license plate—
the invention that
sparked a commitment
to patenting his work.

One of Rowland's
two submissions
to the Packard Motor
Company Design
Competition, 1951.

A connection to Detroit

Rowland had always been passionate about cars, and for a while even contemplated a career in the auto industry. Cranbrook's proximity to Detroit—a mere 20 miles (32 km) away—created access and opportunities. He got a chance to tour the styling department of one of the major car manufacturers in the city, and to apply for a job. Rowland designed three cars while at Cranbrook. Two of these were for a Packard Motor Car Company contest held at the school. Although each industrial design student entered one car, Rowland decided to do two, to cover more bases. He worked on them for months, often staying up until three in the morning. Version Number One was wildly innovative; it had three doors and a gold-anodized aluminum roof and held eight people. Version Number Two was a more traditional car design that modified the hood and fender shapes, but required no new factory tooling. He won no prize, but his effort to do twice the work reveals his energy and commitment. He was accustomed, after his wartime experiences, to pushing himself to full capacity.

One of Rowland's ideas for car design featured a gas cap under the rear license plate, centrally located and neatly hidden—an idea that followed Moholy's mantra of seeing a need, then designing a solution for it. The prior year at USC, when he'd had a job pumping gas, each time a car pulled into the station, he never knew which side had the gas cap, so he'd have to run around the car to see. When interviewing for a summer job at a major motor company, Rowland wanted to make a great impression, so he shared the idea. He didn't get the job, and his interviewers expressed no interest in his gas-cap design. Six months later, however, gas caps began appearing under the license plates of that company's cars. Over the coming decades, 800,000 cars came out with this feature. Rowland never knew whether it was just coincidence or if the company had taken his idea. When friends asked him if he was bitter that his idea was stolen, he would answer, "No. There are more ideas where that one came from." Nonetheless, the experience was a searing lesson in the importance of legally protecting his ideas. From then on, the pursuit of patents became a major part of Rowland's approach to design.

David Rowland: 40/4 Chair

A final project at
Cranbrook. Rowland
designed an office
space, which included
his modern adjustable
hanging light and glass
top desk.

Graduation and first commission

Rowland master's thesis was titled "Form, Deform, and Reform." In the section called "Form," he theorized that ancient humans had a very pure sense of form, proven by functional tools that were beautiful in their simplicity. He pointed to the *adz* his grandfather obtained in the early 1900s from Native Alaskans. "Deform" covered over-ornamentation and over-decoration. Then "Reform" addressed the clean lines, surface, and volume indicated by Bauhaus design, dedicated to function.

In 1951, Rowland graduated from Cranbrook Academy of Art with an MFA in industrial design. At the commencement, the president of the academy, Zoltan Sepeshy, delivered an irreverent speech in the campus recreation room, while smoking cigarettes. He reminded the graduates that they'd be facing tough competition in getting a job. He estimated that there were a hundred design schools in the country, each graduating forty students that year. That meant 4,000 design students all looking for jobs at the same time. "Kiddies," he said, "You don't have a chance! ... May the good Lord kiss you on your cheeks, all four of them, and send you on your way."

Rowland did not leave until August, however, because he had made an agreement with Cranbrook to stay through the summer after graduation so that he could use the school's studio equipment. He'd just received his first seating commission for a bold and experimental chair that he called the Transparent Chair, designed to use S-shaped (sinuous) springs, which were typically employed by carmakers inside auto seats. Rowland brought a one-eighth-scale model to Henry Hopkes Jr., CEO of the Detroit-area No-Sag Spring Company, which specialized in S-springs. Rowland arrived at just the right time. No-Sag had been doing auto seats but wanted to expand to furniture. Hopkes commissioned Rowland to make a prototype of the Transparent Chair, to be featured at the National Home Furnishings Show in New York City. Hopkes even asked Rowland to design the exhibit. By the end of the summer, Rowland completed the prototype. His career had begun, and he was ready to launch.

An Independent Career and Life in New York City

Rowland's first chair
commission, the
Transparent Chair,
marked the beginning
of his decades-
long interest in
sinuous S-springs, a
foundational material
in many of his chair
designs.

With his newly minted MFA degree and his first commission for the Transparent Chair completed, Rowland packed his belongings and left Cranbrook, setting his sights on New York City. His route was indirect, by way of California, because he went home to Stockton to visit his parents and made a side trip to Los Angeles to meet with Charles Eames. By then, Eames was well known for his groundbreaking architecture, furniture designs, and especially his modern chairs.

The meeting must have gone well, because Eames offered Rowland a job. It was a significant opportunity, but one that Rowland ultimately declined because he felt pulled eastward. Ever since he'd started reading design magazines, he noticed that the leading modern design companies were headquartered or had showrooms in New York City. As he saw it, if he stayed in California and worked for Eames, he would ultimately be a California designer. But if he went to New York City, he could become a world designer. Rowland was clear that he wanted to be a world designer, so he drove to New York, where he knew no one, and rented a cramped room for forty dollars a month on Madison Avenue and 94th Street.

Rowland started his career with a bang in 1951, at the annual National Home Furnishings Show, held in Manhattan's opulent Grand Central Palace, where hundreds of companies came each year to present their wares. One of these was the No-Sag Spring Company and its exhibit featuring Rowland's Transparent Chair. The chair captured major media attention with its forward-thinking technology. Journalist Mike Wallace interviewed Rowland on national television, and articles and photos of Rowland and his chair appeared in major newspapers and magazines around the country. The *Christian Science Monitor* ran a photo with the caption, "Designer David Rowland with His 'Chair of Tomorrow.'" It was also called "a chair ahead of its time." For a young designer of just twenty-eight, this was an exciting beginning.

The Transparent Chair was unconventional, fabricated with gold-plated springs that were dipped in clear vinyl and in full view. "I wanted to build a thin chair out of a resilient material in which the design would be as pure and as apparent as possible," Rowland said in one interview, noting that he thought the repeating serpentine shape of the springs was beautiful and deserved to be seen. The Transparent Chair marked the beginning of a decades-long relationship with the sinuous spring—and the No-Sag Spring Company that manufactured them. Rowland embraced these wire springs because they allowed him to create "give" and softness in seating without having to use bulky padding. In common with many of his subsequent designs, the Transparent Chair had a slim profile, only 1/4 in (0.6 cm) thick, and was framed with steel tubing. It was innovative, weatherproof, and elegant. Many of the design ideas he used to build this chair would continue to concern him for years to come, especially its uncluttered and simple structure, emphasizing comfort, function, and beauty.

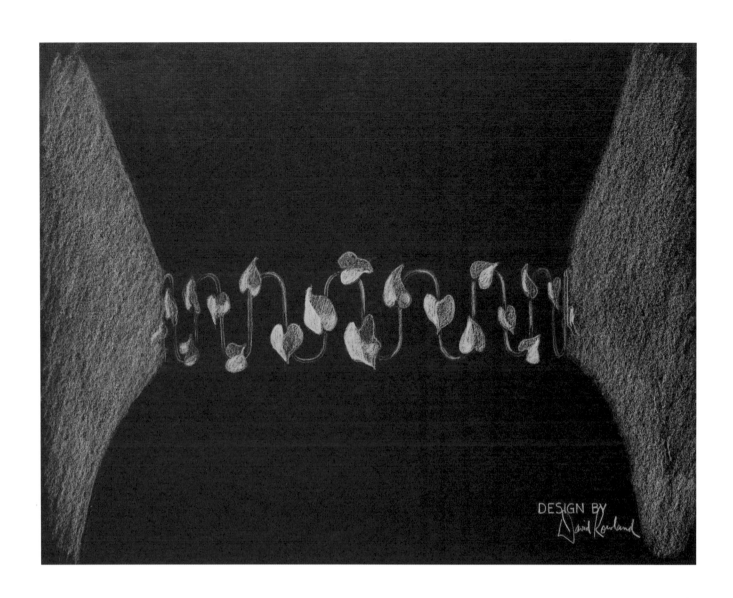

David Rowland: 40/4 Chair

Rowland believed in exploring how existing industrial materials could be used in new ways. S-springs in a series of women's belts, mid-1950s.

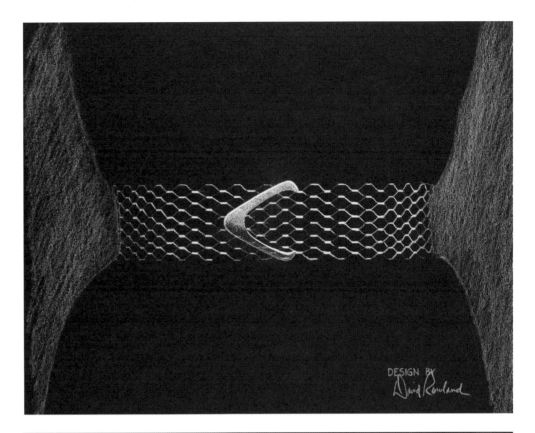

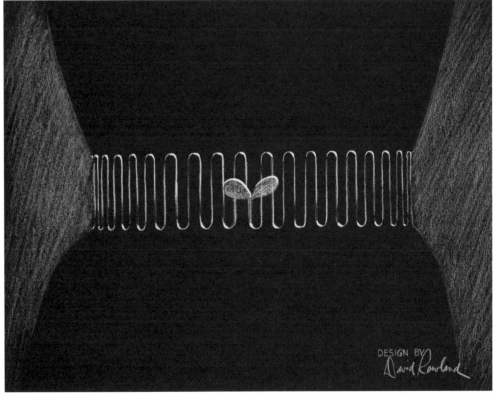

The independent path

When Rowland had arrived in New York City, he'd intended to get a job with an industrial design office or studio—a clear career path for an up-and-coming professional. He interviewed with several firms and received job offers. But when he learned that these firms required him to sign away the rights to his inventions while in their employ, he couldn't agree.

One such offer came from Raymond Loewy, the French-born product designer, branding genius, and businessman described, along with Norman Bel Geddes, as the father of American industrial design. During the 1920s, Loewy had founded a design firm to make products more beautiful, "clean-lined," and stylish. By the early 1950s, his firm had developed the iconic look and feel of hundreds of American brands, ranging from Frigidaire and Studebaker to Coca-Cola, Lucky Strike, and Greyhound buses. To achieve such vast reach, however, Loewy had dozens of uncredited designers and draftsmen working for him. Becoming one of them required a deal Rowland wasn't willing to make.

Rowland decided to forgo a steady income rather than sign away his designs, and instead took on a range of freelance projects to pay the bills, sometimes working around the clock. He worked for the animator and filmmaker Ted Eshbaugh, cutting film strips, and for the Nielsen Company, making graphs of product sales. Nights and weekends, he worked on his own designs, often many at once, at an intense pace. Although he had taken a risk going off on his own, he was energized. He began to seek additional commissions through which he could make his mark.

Lamps, outdoor furniture, and other projects in New York

Rowland's early career coincided with a moment in history when many needs had been neglected during nearly two decades of the Great Depression and World War II. Now, American industry was taking off. New technology and materials were creating possibilities of all types for consumer goods, and an explosion of population and jobs were changing the way people lived, worked, and used space. It was an expansive time, full of opportunity for designers.

Rowland did not limit himself to any one type of design product. He had an interest in lighting, for example, going back to his studies with Moholy. At Cranbrook, as part of his graduate project, he had designed an adjustable hanging chandelier. Shortly after his arrival in New York, he entered it into a contest sponsored by the Illuminating Engineering Society, where it won first prize. He also designed several other lamps, some using mesh filters to diffuse light.

This phase of Rowland's career was also influenced by many remarkable experiences with twentieth-century design visionaries who were changing the way modern life looked and functioned. One of these was Maria Bergson, a trailblazing interior designer, industrial designer, and architect known for revolutionizing the interiors of offices, banks, hotels, hospitals, and stores so that they were more functional and efficient. She also created new kinds of lighting and furnishings, including modular workstations that pioneered the office cubicle, with all equipment and supplies within easy reach.

Bergson met Rowland through mutual contacts and commissioned him to create a one-of-a-kind set of terrace furniture for the headquarters of the Pacific Coast Borax Company in Beverly Hills. Rowland embraced the opportunity and designed a suite of colorful, lightly padded lounge seating with his signature minimal lines and slim frames. He faced a challenge, however, because he'd been hired not only to design but also to fabricate the furniture. He didn't have a company or manufacturing arrangement, so he personally built the pieces by hand with the help of friends, completing the project in 1952 after a lot of time and work. Because it was a one-of-a-kind commission, no royalties followed.

The following year, Rowland continued to develop new designs for outdoor lounge furniture, based on his work for Bergson. He experimented with thin, comfortable cushions, minimal base structures, and simple lines that fit around the human body in a lounging position.

After his initial successes, it became clear to Rowland that his commissions weren't bringing in enough income. Worries about money hung over him, as it did for most people who grew up during the Depression. He decided he wanted to design products that he could license so that he could earn ongoing royalties, rather than one-time payments and commission fees.

Rowland frequently visited the city's furniture showrooms to see what was new and to ask to meet with the heads of furniture companies, so that he could find out what kind of product they needed. In one of these meetings, the president of an established outdoor furniture company said he wanted a waterproof seat cushion, something that didn't exist at the time. No upfront funds were offered, but Rowland took on the challenge, went home, and got to work on it.

Over the next two years, Rowland studied the problems of outdoor cushions and carried out countless experiments. He came up with a completely weatherproof, waterproof, and washable cushion. His design featured loosely woven fabrics, perforated insulation, and padding that allowed water to pass easily through the seat so

Outdoor lounge seating.
The influential
designer Maria Bergson
commissioned Rowland to
design and fabricate a
custom set of terrace
furniture for the
executive offices of
the Pacific Coast Borax
Company in Beverly
Hills, CA, 1952.

Overleaf:
After the Bergson
project, Rowland
continued to explore
outdoor seating,
designing new pieces
with his signature
simple lines and thin,
comfortable seats.

David Rowland: 40/4 Chair

it could dry rapidly, rather than become waterlogged and mildewed. He also coated and rustproofed the springs. Rowland protected his design with a patent. Then he returned to the company and presented his cushion. The president was delighted, said he wanted it, and sent Rowland to the company lawyer to work out the details. The lawyer offered a flat fee of $5,000 for all rights—an enormous sum of money for Rowland. Instead of accepting it, however, he asked for royalties and explained that he wanted to continue to create modern designs for the company. The lawyer said no to royalties, then pointed to a banal-looking plant stand in his office and added, "See that plant stand? I designed it. That's as modern as we're going to get!" Rowland declined the offer and left.

Rowland took the idea to a competitor, Lee Woodard & Sons, a major maker of outdoor patio furniture. Woodard wanted it, and Rowland licensed the product and earned royalties. The product was called the Drain Dry Cushion. Although small, the royalties were enough to cover Rowland's rent for the next fifteen years. In many ways, this deal became the prototype for his path as an independent industrial designer: identify a problem, experiment with materials, find a solution, get patent protection, then license it to a company for royalties.

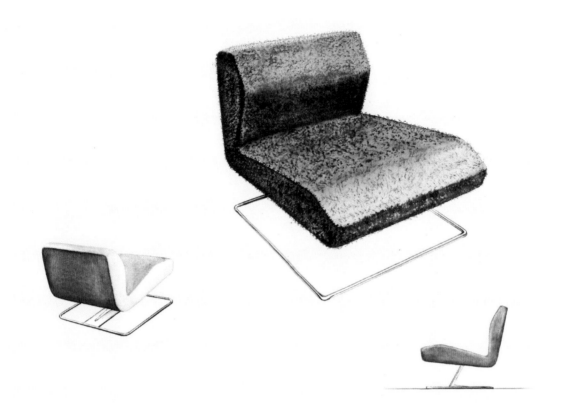

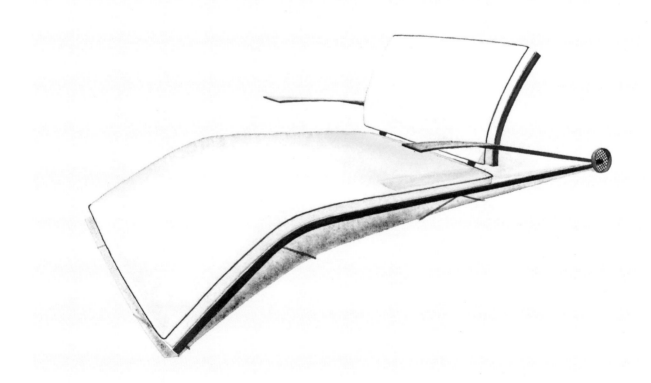

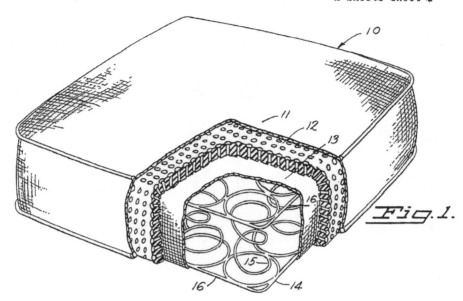

Fig.1.

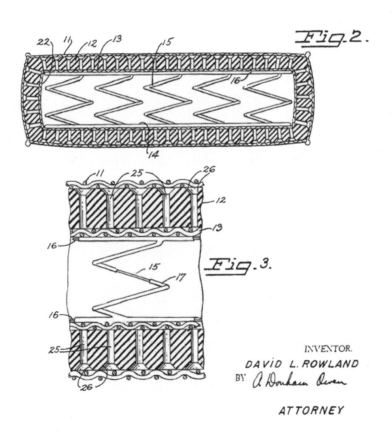

Fig.2.

Fig.3.

INVENTOR.
DAVID L. ROWLAND
BY *A. Donham Owen*

ATTORNEY

March 12, 1957   D. L. ROWLAND   2,784,773

WEATHERPROOF CUSHION

Filed Nov. 23, 1953   2 Sheets-Sheet 2

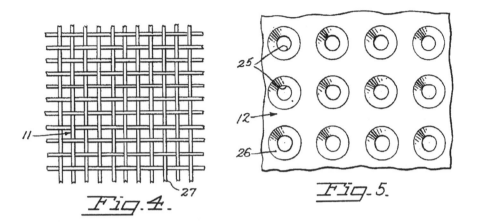

Fig. 4.

Fig. 5.

Patent drawings for
Rowland's Drain
Dry Cushion, which
he licensed to Lee
Woodward & Sons.

After two years of
experimentation,
Rowland invented an
outdoor seat that
allowed water to easily
pass through so the
material could quickly
dry. He licensed it to
Lee Woodward & Sons.
The royalties paid
his rent for the next
fifteen years.

David Rowland: 40/4 Chair

But wire is more than a visualizing medium in the work of David Rowland. It is one of the primary materials to be found in many of his finished designs.

"Steel wire fits a concept which I believe to be fundamental to good design," he explains. *"Accomplish the most with the least.*

"A small amount of wire can furnish great strength with very little weight or bulk. It can provide rigidity, but also resiliency. And wire suggests intriguing visual ideas: its openness, for example, and its literally infinite variety of forms."

While a student at Cranbrook Academy of Art, Rowland was attracted to the beauty of line in an ordinary steel wire, no-sag spring, a type that had been in use for years but was nearly always hidden.

For Rowland, it soon became the curving patternwork of a chair back—strong, resilient, but beautiful in its own right, without upholstering or covering—and the chair was exhibited at the famed *Triennale* exhibition in Milan in 1957.

Designs for seating have occupied much of David Rowland's attention. Even as a student, he experimented with ideas for minimum-thickness chairs that would conserve space without sacrificing comfort.

In a recent project, he set a design discipline of one-half inch stacking

thickness for a stackable, gangable chair made of steel wire rod and vinyl-coated steel sheet, the GF 40/4 chair. It won grand prize as the best single object in the Milan *Triennale,* and was chosen by the Museum of Modern Art for its permanent collection and for the seating of opening night guests.

Rowland regards the disciplines he sets as being central to his work.

"Beauty is achieved by struggling within the framework of disciplines.

"This includes disciplines that the designer chooses as his project goals, and others that are imposed upon him by the realities of nature, or of custom. The stricter the disciplines, and the stricter his adherence to them, the surer he is that the final design will be a good one.

"Cost, for example, is an ever present discipline. Many products could be as good as they are, but cost less, if designers truly and invariably accepted this discipline."

There may be weight and size limitations, production considera-

tions, and particular needs such as a simple means of fastening a product together. And public acceptance functions as a discipline, but this one is a little more subtle.

"The public influences design. So do the manufacturer and the salesman. But the designer must do the designing. When a customer

walks into a store and says, 'I know exactly what I want,' he is wrong. There may be something vastly better than what he has in mind. The manufacturer who says, 'I know what will sell,' and who then attempts to dictate the design, is making the same mistake. The designer who accepts either of these dictates as the final answer might as well leave his drawing board and become a tailor.

"Public acceptance and sales potential are important disciplines, but they must remain an influence on design thinking, not a replacement for it."

The decisive disciplines for each project are those that the designer sets for himself. They define the accomplishment that he is striving

for, and they greatly influence his choice of materials.

A good example is the weatherproof cushion that Rowland recently designed. Essential disciplines: maximum comfort and complete immunity to weather.

Rowland tried every material from fiber glass to redwood bark, plus various methods of encasing spring units in plastic cover seals. Each left something lacking, either in weatherproofness or in comfort.

Finally, he decided to build a unit that would let water go clear through it, rather than attempting to keep the water out. The core consists of a spring wire unit encased under slight compression in an envelope made of potato sacking. This encased spring unit is dipped in a weatherproof coating, then covered with rubberized, curled hog hair and Dacron®-wool fabric. Left out in the rain, the entire cushion simply drains dry, unharmed.

Rowland is now applying the same drain-dry principle to a design for hospital mattresses. For cleaning, the whole mattress can be hosed down, and the water goes down a drain pipe.

"We can do marvelous things with wire if we put our heads to it," Rowland says. *"Again, it is a case of striving to make the most with the least. I use wire a great deal because of its ability to meet this general discipline, and I expect to use it a great deal more."*

←
Rowland with a cross-section of his Drain Dry Cushion, a coil of steel wire in hand, and a scale model of his 40/4 chair on the table.

↑
"Steel wire fits a concept which I believe to be fundamental to good design—to accomplish the most with the least," he said in an interview with *Product Engineering* magazine, 1965.

Architectural drawing
for Norman Bel Geddes.
The renowned industrial
designer hired Rowland
as an architectural
draftsman from 1953
to 1955.

Working for Norman Bel Geddes

In 1953, another mid-century design visionary entered Rowland's life when he got a call out of the blue. Norman Bel Geddes called Cranbrook seeking recommendations for an expert draftsman to create architectural drawings. He was told to call David Rowland. After an interview, he offered Rowland a job—one that didn't require him to sign away rights. Rowland agreed and worked for Bel Geddes two-and-a-half years, able to pursue his own designs on his own time.

Rowland was impressed by the freedom of thought he witnessed in Bel Geddes, who had begun his career as an innovative theatrical director and set designer and later brought his sweeping imagination to the field of industrial design. For more than two decades Bel Geddes had been developing futuristic cars, homes, cities, trains, ocean liners, planes, and consumer goods, popularizing the "streamlining" aesthetic of the prewar period. His "Futurism" exhibit—an amazing panorama of superhighways and interconnected cities envisioned for 1960—had been one of the most popular at the New York World's Fair of 1939.

By the time the two men worked together, Bel Geddes had closed his office and was working out of his Park Avenue apartment. Rowland would go there to discuss and receive his assignments. While there, he had the opportunity to see, at first hand, his boss's out-of-the-ordinary approach, both to design and to life. Among the memorable details: Bel Geddes had many lizards crawling around his apartment and was fascinated by insects. He made a movie about "Ant-ony and Cleopatra," using ants as the main characters, filmed in his bathtub, coaxing them onto a toy boat with bacon grease as bait, and using a fan to sail them across the "Mediterranean" from Italy to Egypt.

What made the greatest impact on Rowland was the experience of working with someone who constantly pursued ideas and designs that hadn't been done before. For example, Rowland rendered Bel Geddes's "Wall-less House," a home designed with walls that could be opened or closed depending on the weather.

In 1955, Bel Geddes took his staff, including Rowland as head draftsman, to Ocho Rios, Jamaica, for the summer. Bel Geddes and his wife, Edith Lutyens, lived in one house and his staff lived in another, where they had a housekeeper and a cook. Rowland worked hard all week but had the evenings and weekends free to enjoy the beaches, culture, and music of Jamaica. That summer he did enough drawings to cover the walls of a room 20 ft (6 m) square, from floor to ceiling. He was an exceptional draftsman, and the architectural renderings he produced during this period were some of his most beautiful, full of depth and precision.

David Rowland: 40/4 Chair

Architectural
renderings of Wall-
less House, designed
with walls that could
be opened or closed
depending on weather,
by David Rowland for
Norman Bel Geddes.

An Independent Career and Life in New York City

David Rowland: 40/4 Chair

Rowland had a lifelong
interest in interior
and architectural
design and embraced
the opportunity to
design an apartment
on Sutton Place in
Manhattan. He chose
simple contemporary
furniture and used
diaphanous screens and
dividers to separate
the space, 1955.

Many types of design

Rowland had diverse design interests, including a love of architecture and interior design dating back to his early childhood, when he roamed Hollyhock House. That is why, when opportunities arose for him to design interiors and architectural projects, he took them not only for financial reasons but also because he was capable and enjoyed this type of work. In 1954, he designed a travel-agency interior at 666 Fifth Avenue and an apartment on Sutton Place. Following the credo of doing the most with the least, he used diaphanous screens and beaded dividers between spaces, and specified simple contemporary furniture. That same year, a friend commissioned him to design the renovation for a home in the Riverdale neighborhood of the Bronx. Rowland's work there shows the influence of Frank Lloyd Wright.

Rowland's parents were always an important part of his life, encouraging and supporting him through letters, phone calls, and occasional visits to New York. His father, as director of the Haggin Museum, often sent him on missions to procure artwork for the museum's collection, especially paintings by J. C. Leyendecker and other illustrators.

In 1956, inspired by these and many other experiences, Rowland invented a new kind of wall system for hanging works of art in museums. His design consisted of a metal mesh underside covered with panels of yarn, which eliminated the need for the museum walls to be repaired and repainted whenever an exhibition changed. It is another example of his approach, in which Rowland saw a need for something, then designed a simple, straightforward product to replace the inefficient way things had previously been done.

Rowland's design for
an architectural
renovation of a house
in Riverdale, NY,
evokes the aesthetic
of Frank Lloyd Wright,
an early childhood
influence, 1954.

Rowland designed
this simple but
ingenious Museum Wall
System in 1956. A mesh
panel—hidden behind
an attractive panel
of yarn—provides a
structure for hanging
artwork without
putting any hardware
into walls.

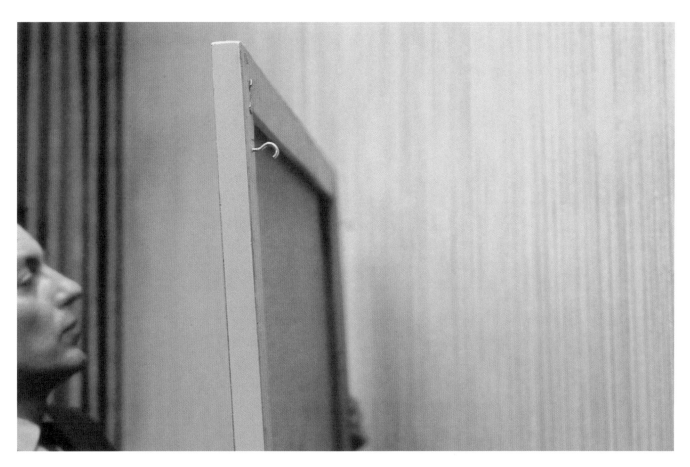

David Rowland: 40/4 Chair

9/16 55 or
Drawn
Aluminum
Tubing.

41 B

Two of Rowland's many
chair designs from
the early 1950s
reveal his endless
experimentation with
the shapes of backs,
seats, and frames.

←
Chair 41A he described
as "a thoroughly
practical design,"
though the frame would
probably need to be
cut and welded. One can
see the lines of the
40/4 Chair taking shape
in this design.

↑
Chair 41B later evolved
into the Zig Zag
Cantilever Chair.

David Rowland: 40/4 Chair

A deep passion for chairs

All the while, chairs remained Rowland's foremost passion. What he really wanted to do was to develop products that could be mass produced, so that the greatest possible number of people could benefit. Chairs could achieve this goal.

Rowland was always working on chair designs, constantly exploring new ways of making seating more comfortable and of making chair frames, seats, and backs that were functional and minimal in design. He crafted scale models out of wire and paper so that he could study the designs in three dimensions. In fact, he kept a roll of wire and pliers beside his bed, so that he could form any ideas that came to him in the middle of the night.

Finding companies to license his work was a job in itself. When Rowland heard that the furniture designer and maker Jens Risom was representing designers to his many contacts in the industry, Rowland called him; it would be a relief to hand over the selling to someone else and focus on the creative work. Risom said he'd be happy to represent Rowland in exchange for substantial percentage of royalties, which Rowland found to be too large. He decided he would just have to continue to approach furniture companies himself.

In 1955, Rowland showed his Zig Zag Cantilever Chair to Hans Knoll, founder of Knoll Associates, one of the very few manufacturers of modern furniture at that time. Knoll was enthusiastic and told Rowland he wanted the chair, saying that he would make a deal as soon as he returned from a trip to Cuba. The deal never happened because Knoll died on that trip in a car accident at age forty-one.

This was not the end of Rowland's experiences with Knoll Associates, however. Later, he would call on Hans's wife, Florence, who took over the company, setting up appointments to show her his work. Nor would it be the end of the Zig Zag Cantilever Chair, which Rowland later entered into the 11th Milan Triennale, where it was awarded a diploma. (It also won first prize in a contest sponsored by the National Cotton Batting Institute.) Unfortunately, the chair was never produced. When Rowland submitted his prototype to another company for consideration, the company lost it. The time, difficulty, and expense of building another prototype would have been so great that Rowland just kept moving forward, developing other designs—including his 40/4 Chair, which he had started by then.

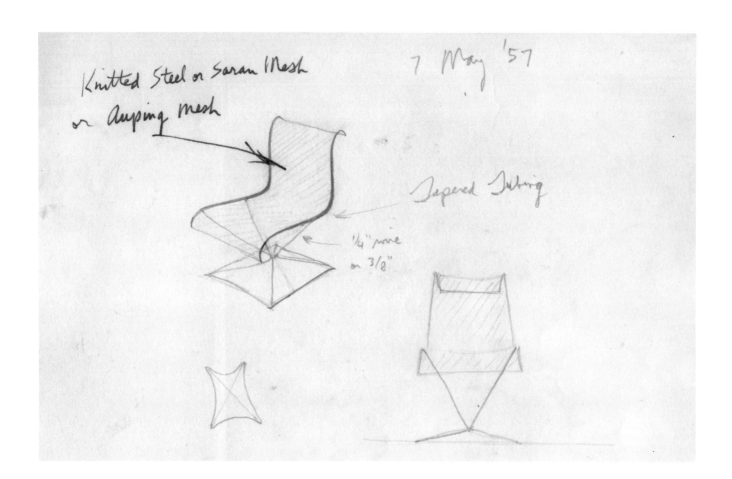

Knitted Steel or Saran Mesh
or Auping Mesh

7 May '57

Tapered Tubing

1/4" more
or 3/8"

David Rowland: 40/4 Chair

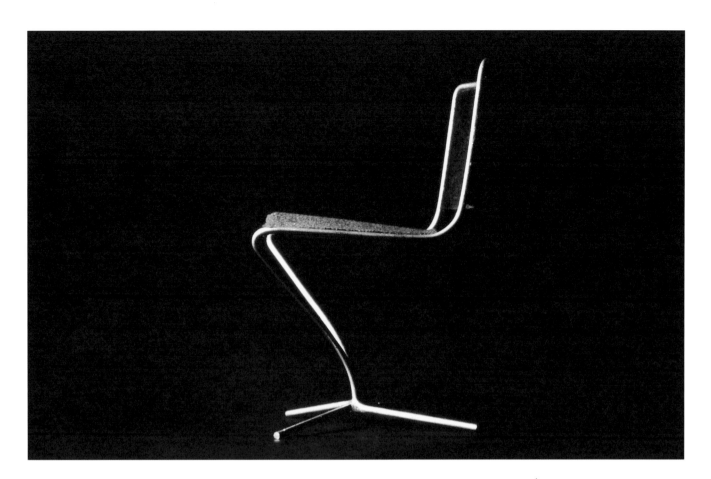

↑
Model of Mesh Chair,
designed with woven
mesh stretched across
a tubular steel frame.

←
Sketches for the
experimental Mesh
Chair, May 1957.

Life in New York City

In the fall of 1955, Rowland left his rented room on Madison Avenue for his own apartment at 49 West 55th Street, half a block from Fifth Avenue. His apartment was on the top floor of a five-floor walk-up (which he never complained about, saying it gave him exercise). It was just two blocks from the Museum of Modern Art (MoMA), which became his backyard, his club, and his inspirational space. For a small fee, he bought a yearly membership that allowed him to go to the museum any time—and he did—to take in the art and design, the sculpture garden and fountain, restaurant, members' lounge, and Monet's Water Lilies gallery, where he sat for long periods contemplating the work. MoMA was his home away from home. He also attended the Christian Science Church on Park Avenue and 63rd Street, which was a sanctuary for him and a place of peace where he could be quiet and "listen for ideas" from the Divine Mind.

Although these early years were a time of hard work and little money, they were also a wonderful period for Rowland, who loved the vibrancy of New York City and embraced all the art and culture it had to offer. He met fascinating people and made friends with artists, architects, actors, and singers. Most had little money but were trying to make their mark, as he was. Rowland had a girlfriend who wrote letters "from a poor struggling model in Dallas to a poor struggling industrial designer in New York." He ice-skated in Central Park, went to concerts, and visited machine shops on the Lower East Side and Hell's Kitchen. Every New Year's Eve for many years, a member of the Haggin Museum's board gave Rowland tickets for his box at the Metropolitan Opera and the use of his chauffeured limousine so Rowland could take his friends to the opera.

In the early 1950s, Rowland first met Bucky Fuller, the architect, industrial designer, inventor, and philosopher (among other things), best known for his geodesic dome. One day, Rowland looked up Fuller's number in the telephone book and called him. Fuller, who lived in Forest Hills in New York City at the time, answered the phone, and the two had a great conversation, talking for more than an hour. Rowland invited Fuller to speak at his father's museum and Fuller agreed. It was the beginning of an important friendship.

Rowland obtained Fuller's schedule of lectures and attended whenever he could, whether in New York City, Boston, or Pennsylvania. As the years went on, they got to know each other more. Rowland also came to know Shoji Sadao, who worked in Long Island City and was Fuller's close friend and architectural partner on the geodesic dome.

Fuller was a visionary who called upon designers to create new structures, systems, and processes that did more with less, so that all people on Earth could have shelter, food, and transportation. Over the years, he provided encouragement for Rowland's work. In many ways the two men were kindred spirits who shared much of the same design philosophy. Both were following their own paths, contrary to the traditional way of doing things. Both brought a spiritual vision to design. Rowland subscribed completely to Fuller's goal: "To make the world work for 100 percent of humanity in the shortest possible time through cooperation without ecological offense or the disadvantage of anyone." He agreed with Bucky's belief that a single individual could contribute to changing the world and benefiting all humanity. These values spoke to Rowland's own conclusions, and would validate, strengthen, and inspire his own approach during the years ahead.

As was typical of New York, there were interesting and surprising experiences with famous people. One day, while walking along upper Fifth Avenue, Rowland saw Frank Lloyd Wright in his pork-pie hat, standing on the street watching the Guggenheim Museum being built.

Rowland also had a chance meeting with Norman Rockwell, the *Saturday Evening Post* cover artist. It was a remarkable encounter because of a prior communication. Earl Rowland had recently been in touch with Rockwell to request that he contribute an introduction to a book Earl was writing on Leyendecker—another *Post* artist, and one whom Rockwell deeply admired. Rockwell was agreeable, but Earl wasn't convinced he would do it. And so, he had asked his son to drive up to see Rockwell at his studio in Stockbridge, Massachusetts, to clinch his commitment. Rowland, who was very busy trying to launch his career, later admitted, "I was a bit lax in getting up there."

The problem was solved when Rowland entered an art supply store just off Fifth Avenue, at the exact moment a pipe-smoking figure was exiting. Seeing that the clerks were all staring, he asked if it was Norman Rockwell. The clerks said yes. Rowland raced back out to the sidewalk and introduced himself as the son of Earl Rowland, who had been in communication about Leyendecker. Then he offered to take Rockwell to lunch at MoMA. Rockwell agreed. Afterward, they went to the print room. Rowland expected that Rockwell would want to look at realistic works, but instead, he asked to see Henri Matisse's *Jazz*. It was a folio of twenty screen prints of cutouts with circus and theater figures, all in brightly contrasting colors amid vibrant activity—anything but Rockwell sentimentality. Rowland later recalled Rockwell's enthusiasm for the piece, and his yearning words, "I wish I could just play in art like this." The moment made a lasting impression. From then on, Rowland held on to the idea of "playing in art" as one of his important aims.

The 40/4 Chair:
A Story of Persistence and
Revolutionary Design

Rowland with a scale
model of a 40/4 Chair.

Throughout the 1950s, Rowland was constantly designing new chairs, working out his concepts in sketches and small three-dimensional wire models. He had plenty of designs, but he needed companies to license and produce them. At the time, he knew of only two, Knoll and Herman Miller, that were manufacturing avant-garde furniture. Both collaborated with the most famous modern chair designers of the era. These companies were where Rowland wanted his work to be.

Early on, Rowland wrote the president of the Herman Miller Company to ask for an appointment and was referred to George Nelson, head of the design department. Nelson declined to meet with him, explaining in a letter in 1954 that the company was already busy producing its own designers' work, and that "the company's interest would hardly be served by the addition of further designs from outside sources."

If the door was instantly shut at Herman Miller, Rowland had the opposite experience at Knoll, where he found the door was open, and stayed open, for years. Florence Knoll had taken the helm of the company after her husband, Hans, died in 1955. While he was the charismatic businessman, she was the design visionary who had studied under or hired such mid-century luminaries as Ludwig Mies van der Rohe, Eero Saarinen, Marcel Breuer, and Walter Gropius. At Knoll, she had pioneered the Knoll Planning Unit, which created office interiors for the largest American corporations, and she also commissioned, or herself designed, some of the most iconic furnishings of the twentieth century.

Rowland had never met Florence Knoll. However, she, like Rowland, was a graduate of Cranbrook Academy of Art, and he thought, based on that connection, she might be willing to see him. He was right. When he called and asked for an appointment, Knoll agreed. He arrived at the showroom with a scale model of one of his chairs, this one made of wood, an idea he had worked on for many months. He put the model in her hands. Knoll took it, studied it, and critiqued it patiently, but then she handed it back to him, saying, "We wouldn't be interested."

Knoll was so encouraging and gracious that Rowland saw this meeting as a beginning, rather than an end. Over the next two or three months, he developed another chair design that he thought would surely meet her requirements. When it was ready, he called and made another appointment. Once again, Mrs. Knoll (as he called her) was gracious, studied the new model, and critiqued it conscientiously. Once again, she turned him down. Rowland went home and worked on another design, again spending months crafting a model he thought she would like. When he was finished, he called for yet another appointment. And, once again, she gave him kind and thoughtful criticism—along with a rejection.

george nelson

george nelson and associates

George Nelson, A.I.A.

Irving Harper

William C. Renwick

John F. Pile

30 West 57th Street, New York 19, N. Y., JUdson 2-0260

April 22, 1954

Mr. David Rowland
1326 Madison Avenue
New York, New York

Dear Mr. Rowland:

I have just received your letter which arrived shortly after discussions both at the factory and with the Sales Department.

It is our feeling that it would be better if you continued development of the chair independently and made arrangements with No-Sag and perhaps some suitable distributor.

The Herman Miller problem with regard to your chairs is pretty much what it has been for the past several years: the output of the Eames office and our own has already strained the company's facilities, and it is the general feeling that the company's interest would hardly be served by the addition of further designs from outside sources.

I appreciate your taking the trouble to bring up the models and hope you will be successful in finding a satisfactory distribution.

si Sincerely,

GN:ML

Product Design   Architecture   Graphic Design   Prototype Research

September 20, 1957

Mr. David Rowland
49 West 55
New York 19, New York

Dear Mr. Rowland:

Thank you for your letter of September 11.

We are interested in seeing the chair which you have developed.
I regret, however, that I have no immediate plans for being in
New York. May I suggest, therefore, that you contact Mr. John
Pile, c/o George Nelson and Associates, 18 East 50th Street,
New York, New York, who I am sure would also like to see this
chair.

As you perhaps know, Mr. George Nelson is in charge of our
entire design program. It is his responsibility to approve
designs from others that we might consider for production.

We are sending a copy of this letter to Mr. Pile and he will
undoubtedly be waiting to hear from you.

Yours truly,

HERMAN MILLER FURNITURE COMPANY

Hugh De Pree
tdh
cc:John Pile

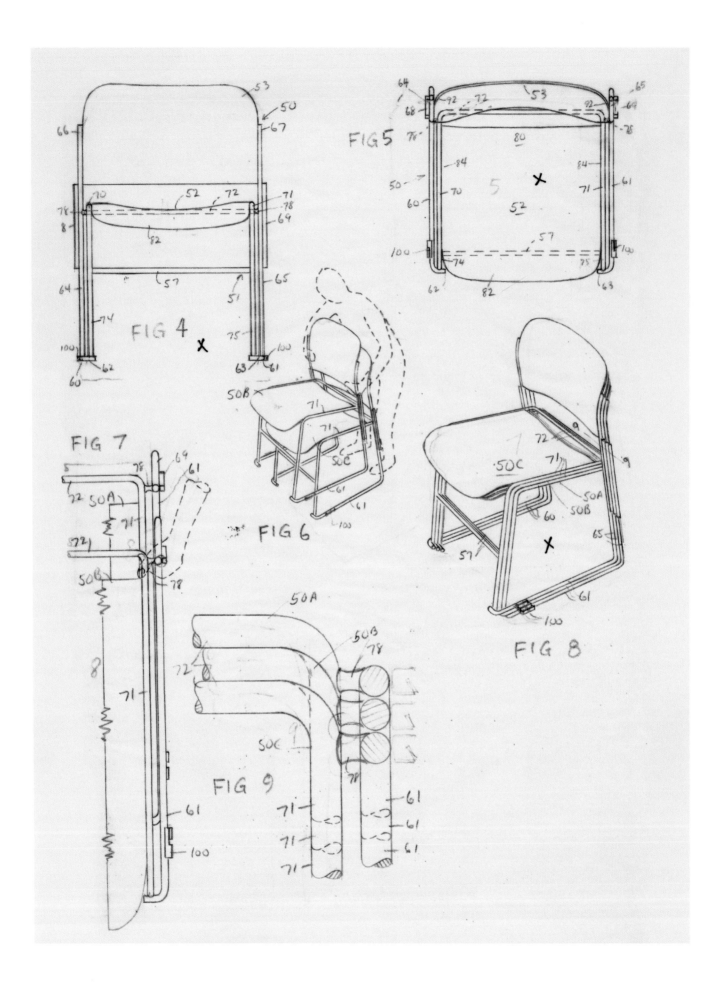

FIG 4

FIG5

FIG 7

FIG 6

FIG 8

FIG 9

David Rowland: 40/4 Chair

←
A Compactly Stackable
Chair, technical
drawing from the patent
application, granted
in 1963.

May 8, 1961

Mr. David Rowland
49 West 55th Street
New York, N. Y.

Dear Mr. Rowland:

We write to confirm our mutual understanding that the
agreement between us dated November 18, 1958 be,
and it hereby is, terminated in all respects as of the
date hereof without either of us being in any way
under any obligation or liability to the other.

Very truly yours,

KNOLL ASSOCIATES INC.

W. Cornell Dechert
President

WCD:dm

Agreed and Accepted

This_____Day of_____ 1961

_____

An idea Florence Knoll couldn't refuse

After years of trying to win over Knoll with his chair designs, Rowland became frustrated. Each model he built took months and expense. How many times could he pour his heart into creating a chair design, only to have her turn it down? He decided to take a break and reconsider his approach.

After some reflection, he concluded that he must stop trying to appeal to (or outguess) Florence Knoll's (or indeed anyone's) taste. As he later described in an interview with the *Christian Science Monitor*, he understood that he "had to go much deeper than surface effect." He had to include "a certain redefinition of a chair and what it must do for people. It had to be not just different, but clearly better." In fact, it must be so much better than anything anyone had ever seen before, that she wouldn't be able to resist. Or, as he later described it, "I must do such a good job that it would be like a pistol to her head, an offer she couldn't refuse." This meant he would have to design a chair that offered added features.

Rowland returned to his idea of a compactly stackable chair, his 40/4 , which had been on the back burner for a few years while he worked on other projects. Now it was clear that this would be the chair he would bring Knoll. This would be the one she couldn't refuse. He revisited and perfected the design, honing every detail of its form and function: to save space while offering unprecedented comfort. He reworked the angles of the seat, the lumbar curve of the back, the frame, and the quality of materials.

When the design was finished, Rowland knew that this time, a small-scale model wouldn't do; he would have to present Knoll with two full-size chairs so that she could sit on them and fully experience the function of his design. That meant building two prototypes—a time-consuming and very expensive process, and one for which he didn't have the facilities or tools. At a machine shop on the Lower East Side, he found a German immigrant who rented him space and tools by the hour. It was a painstaking and challenging process. Thirty-two iterations later, he was ready with his prototypes.

He called Knoll and set up an appointment, this time arriving with a pair of his full-size 40/4 Chairs, stacked and so slim they appeared as one. When she entered the showroom, Rowland presented his new seating design and invited her to sit on it. She did. Then, when she stood up, he lifted off the top chair, revealing that she had actually been sitting on two chairs. Within fifteen seconds, she said, "We'll take it."

Knoll offered Rowland a contract with a flat fee of $20,000 for world rights and a plan to produce 5,000 chairs a year. It was a thrilling development for him after so many years—not to mention that he needed the money. But he resisted. He wanted a royalty arrangement, not a once-and-done fee. Knoll agreed. Finally, he'd achieved his dream, a moment that he later described as "the happiest thing that ever happened in my whole life." Rowland's 40/4 Chair was under contract with Knoll in November 1958, and he began working with the company's engineers to plan production. A letter dated January 1961 spelled out Knoll's final approval.

And yet, it was not to be. In a letter dated May 1961, Knoll canceled the contract. Rowland never fully understood why. At least two vice presidents had been clear that they wanted the chair, and Rowland wondered if interior politics had shifted the tide. After coming so close to success, now he was back where he'd started, with a design he believed in but no one to license and manufacture it.

THE DAVID ROWLAND STACKING CHAIR

PATENTS PENDING

Cover for Rowland's
self-produced sales
brochure. He sent it to
furniture manufacturers
around the world in
English and French
versions, trying to
gain interest.

Rowland's self-
produced brochures
illustrated the chair's
unique features,
including compactness,
portability, ganging,
and comfort.

Rejection and redirection

With a turndown at Knoll and a closed door at Herman Miller, Rowland needed another plan. In the weeks that followed, he sent out letters and photos pitching the chair and its unique features to office furniture companies of many different kinds. Everyone turned him down. He developed presentation brochures, including one with English and French language versions, to send to companies around the world. At each turn, he met with either rejection or no response at all.

The 40/4 was so innovative and different that furniture companies couldn't see its possibilities. It was just too futuristic and unconventional looking, and they doubted the strength and durability of such a lightweight and slim design. As Bucky Fuller explained in his writing and speeches, it was normal and to be expected that there would be a "gestational lag" between the emergence of an invention and its acceptance." Rowland took heart in this idea, hoping that eventually, buyers would understand that the 40/4 Chair was not only extremely strong but also beautiful and filled a vast untapped need. Or, as Rowland's father noted in 1959 in a letter to his son:

> As for your stacking chairs: I am often reminded of how valuable a help they would be even in our smallish museum right now, for we have to fold and place, then fold again and stack, all of the chairs that are used in the Sunday after-noon concerts we are now having each week. These chairs take too much room and are heavy and slow to handle. Yours will be light and quick and far better in appearance than these. These have sold by the millions, perhaps yours will sell by the tens of millions!

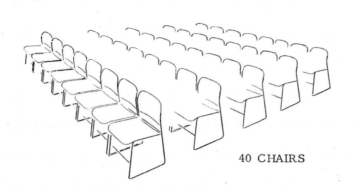 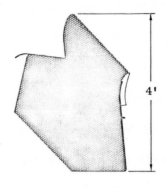

40 CHAIRS

COMPACTNESS

In quantities above ten, this design places more chairs in a given volume than has ever before been achieved with either folding or stacking chairs. Forty chairs can be stacked into a height of approximately four feet! In larger quantities the net occupation of space averages 2 chairs per cubic foot! (i.e., 240 chairs will go into 120 cubic feet.)

PORTABILITY

The individual chair is light in weight, and in quantities can be carried easily on dolly-carts. This will make it possible for two men to stack or place in an auditorium as many as 500 chairs in 5 to 10 minutes!

David Rowland: 40/4 Chair

GANGING

Another important feature of this design is that each chair can be strongly fastened to the next with a specially designed and patent-protected fastening system. The advantage of this is that it provides for the easy stacking of rows of chairs onto rows of chairs, with the same compactness as stacking single chairs, a feature never before accomplished. No tools or extra parts are needed.

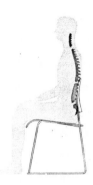

COMFORT

The primary objective of any chair design must be comfort. This project has been thoroughly studied, built and rebuilt many times to achieve a high level of comfort in hard-surface seating. The back has been a special object of this study and it achieves a maximum of comfort for either slouched loungers or the upright sitter. It is appropriately suited to auditoriums and theatres and other places where people sit for hours at a time.

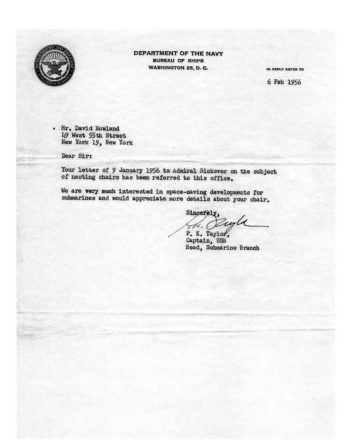

↑
Rowland approached the
U.S. Navy, reasoning
that his compact
stackable chair would
be useful in the
limited spaces of
submarines and ships.
He received interest
but was told to come
back when he had a
manufacturer.

→
The note Davis Allen
at Skidmore, Owings &
Merrill (SOM), gave
Rowland sending him
to see Art Stuckey at
GF. It was the "key"
that opened the door to
the company that would
license and manufacture
the 40/4 Chair.

Turning point: Skidmore, Owings & Merrill

By the end of 1962, Rowland reached a low point from all the rejection and indifference. Not long afterward, he went to a contemporary furniture show at the New York Coliseum. He'd always enjoyed these events, where he could see new designs on display and meet people in the business. Walking through the show, he started to go down one aisle when he spotted Knoll's vice president, Chuck Shepherd, who had negotiated the contract for the 40/4 at Knoll. Rowland's first inclination was to keep going and avoid the man associated with a company that had canceled his contract. But a voice in his head told him to go down the aisle and meet him. So he did, and offered a handshake, asking Shepherd how he was. Shepherd replied that he was out of a job; Knoll had let him go. He then expressed his support for the 40/4 Chair and offered advice. He told Rowland that instead of pitching to companies that manufactured furniture, he should approach architectural firms that specified it. The advice came with a referral. Shepherd told him to see Davis Allen, head of interior design at the world-class architecture firm Skidmore, Owings & Merrill (SOM).

Rowland immediately made an appointment with Allen, who took one look at the 40/4 Chair and expressed enthusiasm. He said he wanted it for a major project. His firm was designing the new Chicago Circle Campus for the University of Illinois and needed a great number of chairs, and Allen thought the 40/4 would be perfect. With this meeting, wheels were set in motion for an astonishing order of 17,000 chairs.

Now Rowland just needed a manufacturer. Allen gave him a note with the contact information for Art Stuckey, general manager of sales at General Fireproofing Company (GF), an unlikely prospect for Rowland's sophisticated Bauhaus-inspired design. Rowland made an appointment with Stuckey.

GF was founded in 1902 in Youngstown, Ohio—the heart of steel country—to produce fireproof construction materials. Now it was the largest producer of office and school furniture in the United States, known for making battle-worthy steel desks, filing cabinets, safes, shelving, and metal lathing. This was a high-capacity manufacturing powerhouse. It was also 400 miles (644 km), and a universe, away from Manhattan's design elite. Rowland knew nothing of the company, but he was intrigued by GF's fireproofing and metal expertise because his design for the 40/4 was, after all, both fireproof and built of metal.

A GF label from the
underside of the seat
of a 40/4 Chair.
Rowland's signature
is on every authentic
40/4 Chair.

David Rowland: 40/4 Chair

Licensing the chair: General Fireproofing Company

As Allen instructed, Rowland met Stuckey, who then brought him to meet GF's president, John Saunders. The timing couldn't have been better; GF had just opened a new factory in Forest City, North Carolina, and with all that new capacity, it needed new products to build.

Saunders no doubt saw the very significant upside of licensing a product that had an existing order of 17,000 units to start with. Nonetheless, it required a leap. The factory needed expensive steel dies to form the steel seats and backs of the chairs, and Saunders would have to invest major resources to ensure a high-quality job, setting up production at the new plant and spending hundreds of thousands of dollars in tooling and engineering talent.

Negotiations got underway, and Rowland scheduled another meeting on the agreement. But then a major event happened: his father died, and Rowland had to cancel the meeting and fly to California to bury the man who had never stopped encouraging him from the time he was born. After the funeral, Rowland inherited his father's car and set off to make the long drive back east to New York City. He rescheduled the meeting so he could stop in Ohio on his way and arrived at GF after days of nonstop driving, aware that now, if he succeeded, his loving, supportive father wouldn't be alive to see it.

It would take another couple of months of negotiations, but in November 1963, GF and Rowland signed a licensing agreement for GF to produce the 40/4 Chair. Here was Rowland's breakthrough, finally.

For the first half of 1964 Rowland worked closely with the engineers to produce the chairs and solve challenges that arose. For example, just as production was ready to start, a chair was dropped on the factory floor and broke. Saunders, who happened to be there at the time, stopped production. Everything came to a halt until the engineers figured out what caused it. Happily, it wasn't anything major; a small design change fixed the problem, and the production line began to roll.

The time arrived to unveil the chair to the GF sales team, who came from across the country to the new factory. To build excitement about the product, GF hired a glamorous female model to dramatically push a whole stack of 40/4 chairs to the front of the room on Rowland's specially invented dolly. When the salespeople saw the stack of forty chairs, they jumped to their feet, whooped, hollered, screamed, and whistled. They'd never seen anything like it. Instantly, they were on board and ready to sell. As the years passed, stories and lore accumulated about GF salespeople's enthusiasm for selling the 40/4, including one man who frequently called on schools and requested to be taken to the roof, from where he would throw a chair to the ground to prove its durability.

The alliance between Rowland and GF turned out to be wonderful and productive. The first full year alone brought 50,000 40/4 Chairs into the world—ten times what Knoll had planned. The chair was a huge success, giving the company a high-performing product to build, sell, and promote for years to come.

Rowland later reflected that Knoll probably wouldn't have had the equipment or capacity to produce the chair. He also noted that when he shifted his thinking from his original focus on just two modern furniture companies, a much bigger path opened.

GF40/4

David Rowland: 40/4 Chair

←
The first order for the
40/4 Chair came when
the architectural firm
of Skidmore, Owings &
Merrill (SOM) specified
17,000 chairs for
the new University of
Illinois Chicago Circle
(UIC) campus.

↑
A big splash at the
first sales conference.
GF hired a glamorous
model to help introduce
the 40/4 Chair to its
sales team, 1964.

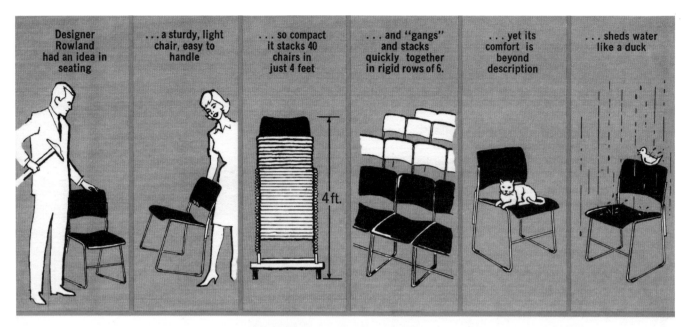

Designer Rowland had an idea in seating

...a sturdy, light chair, easy to handle

...so compact it stacks 40 chairs in just 4 feet

4 ft.

...and "gangs" and stacks quickly together in rigid rows of 6.

...yet its comfort is beyond description

...sheds water like a duck

GF 40/4 CHAIR

designed exclusively for GF by David Rowland

The designer of the GF 40/4 Chair, David Rowland, is a native of Stockton, California, where his father was Director of Haggin Museum and a well-known artist. After graduating from the Cranbrook Academy of Art with an MFA in Industrial Design, he became assistant to Norman Bel Geddes in New York City. Eventually, Mr. Rowland opened his own studio and has devoted a great deal of his energy to seating and its problems. Two of his chairs, including the GF 40/4, have been accepted as representative designs for the American display at the famed Italian Triennale.

PERFECTLY SUITED TO AN ENDLESS VARIETY OF USES...

... in airports

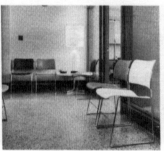

...in doctors' offices

... in hotels and motels

... in banks

... in lunch rooms

... in auditoriums

... in beauty and barber shops

... in bowling alleys

GF THE GENERAL FIREPROOFING COMPANY • YOUNGSTOWN, OHIO 44501

Form No. 422IC964

Copyright 1964 by The General Fireproofing Company, Youngstown, Ohio 44501

Litho in USA

General Specifications

GF 40/4 CHAIR

designed by David Rowland

The GF 40/4 stacking and ganging chair has been designed primarily for comfort, and every angle and contour has been studied carefully to achieve this goal. Built of steel rod and formed metal seat and back, the chair is free of sharp or rough edges and is extremely easy to handle. It weighs approximately thirteen pounds.

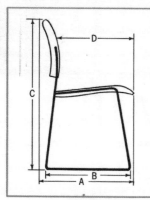

Side elevation

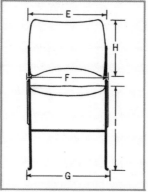

Front elevation

A	22-¼″		D	17-½″		G	19-¼″
B	17-⅝″		E	20-⅛″		H	10-¼″
C	30″		F	16-¹³⁄₁₆″		I	17″

FRAME The 40/4 chair frame is fabricated from ⁷⁄₁₆-inch steel rod possessing all the physical qualities necessary to assure ample strength and rigidity. The back panel support, rear leg, floor rail, front leg and side seat rail are all formed from a single rod. The rear seat rail, which follows the contour of the rear edge of the seat panel, is securely attached to the rear leg where it is joined by the side seat rail. The front cross member is likewise attached securely to the front legs without use of exposed fasteners. The rear legs are further strengthened by integral stiffening members designed to restrict lateral sway and provide a means of ganging or joining in rigid rows.

SEAT AND BACK PANELS Both pans are of formed metal. They have been contoured to fit the body as precisely as possible to provide optimum comfort for tall or short persons over extended periods of time. These panels have a ³⁄₁₆-inch beaded rim-edge for safe handling and improved appearance.

GLIDES Four durable plastic glides snap on by hand and are fastened with a specially designed permanent gripper to the floor rails by a concealed mechanical method.

FRAME FINISHES The frame may be finished in mirror nickel chrome plating or with vinyl coating. Both surfaces are highly resistant to scratching and marring and will provide many years of virtually maintenance-free service.

SEAT AND BACK FINISH The surface finish is a baked-on vinyl and may be either textured or smooth. It is highly durable, resists abrasion, eliminates danger of cigarette burns and cleans easily with naphtha or similar cleaners.

COLORS The GF 40/4 Chair is available in five standard colors: Eggshell, Charcoal Black, Leather Brown, American Vermilion and Royal Purple.

WELDING All frame members and seat and back pans are joined by silver brazing for extra strength to form lasting, exceptionally durable joints.

The GF 40/4 Chair's beauty is derived largely from the graceful curve of its lines and its perfect balance. Its unseen beauty, however, is in its almost unbelievable comfort.

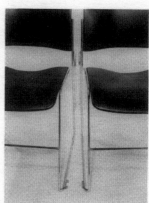

Forty chairs can be stacked on a special dolly in a height of just four feet and four inches; full stack is 22½ inches wide and 36 inches deep overall. Photo at right shows locking devices on rear legs and floor rails.

One man can set up—or restack—forty chairs in minutes. The unique ganging devices illustrated above permit joining of chairs together into rigid rows that can be stacked without unganging.

David Rowland: 40/4 Chair

Rowland stacking
40/4 Chairs on a dolly
at New York City's
Museum of Modern Art
(MoMA), which ordered
250 chairs for the
opening of a new
wing and garden in
May 1964, marking the
chair's debut.

First orders: University of Illinois and Museum of Modern Art

All through 1964, GF charged ahead to fulfill the massive order for the University of Illinois, Chicago Circle Campus. Meanwhile, even before the first chair was completed, word got out, and orders started to arrive.

One of the first came from the prominent New York City architect Philip Johnson, who wanted it for a highly prestigious project his firm was working on. The Museum of Modern Art (MoMA) was completing a major expansion, featuring a new wing and enlarged sculpture garden. Johnson specified 250 of the chairs, to be delivered in time for the opening event in May 1964. This positive development also created a challenge. The factory had only just tooled up and begun producing the separate parts of the chair. Assembly had not yet started. To meet the request from MoMA, GF quickly welded the 250 seats, backs, and frames together by hand and delivered the chairs on time. As a result, on May 25, 1964, the 40/4 had its first public appearance. The chairs were initially placed in the Founder's Room and library, and later appeared throughout the museum. MoMA also added the chair to its permanent collection.

For the 40/4 Chair to debut at MoMA was a spectacular endorsement of Rowland's invention as a useful item, an example of innovative modern design, and a beautiful work of art. It was a personal dream come true, too. MoMA was not only one of the most influential modern art museums in the world, but also a very meaning-ful place for Rowland. From his first days in New York City, the museum had been an important part of his life. It was where he'd experienced rejection and triumph, and it was a place that had held his hopes. Now the museum would also hold the chair he'd worked on for so many years in his walk-up apartment just a few blocks away.

Edgar J. Kaufmann Jr.
presents Rowland with
the coveted Grand
Prix for his 40/4
Chair at the 13th
Milan Triennale, 1964,
a global competition
for innovative
art, design, and
architecture. The award
opened a floodgate of
international orders.

Success, awards, and meeting Edgar Kaufmann Jr. ten years later

As soon as it was released, the 40/4 Chair became a success. In the spring of 1964, the chair was entered for the Milan Triennale, the thirteenth iteration of the famous international exhibition and contest that featured some of the world's newest in industrial design, architecture, and decorative arts. Submissions came from North America, Europe, Japan, and Brazil. Media and design professionals around the world watched the event closely and with great anticipation.

Each participating nation had its own Triennale Committee to evaluate entries. In a twist of fate for Rowland, the United States committee was headed by none other than Edgar Kaufmann Jr., the former curator and head of architecture and design at MoMA. This was the influential man who had given Rowland no hope ten years earlier when he'd arrived at Kaufmann's MoMA office seeking advice and encouragement for his stacking chair. The committee that chose Rowland's chair was filled with elite design and media people, museum curators, and engineering professionals. One of these was George Nelson, the Herman Miller Company's head of design, who had also closed the door on Rowland years earlier, and Cornell Dechert, president of Knoll Associates, who signed the letter canceling Rowland's contract.

The 40/4 Chair won the grand prize, the Grand Prix, for the entire exhibition. This was one of the world's most prestigious awards for industrial design and constituted extraordinary recognition for Rowland's work. The only other American up to that time to have won it was Bucky Fuller, for his geodesic dome at the 11th Triennale in 1957. Receiving the same award as his greatly admired friend only increased the honor for Rowland.

The ceremony was held in New York City. It was Kaufmann who shook Rowland's hand and presented him with the award, expressing wholehearted support, and noting that during four-and-a-half hours of jury deliberations, the chair was so comfortable that he'd had to give it his vote.

In 1964, the American Institute of Interior Designers (AID) gave the 40/4 Chair its annual design award. Four years later, the Austrian government awarded Rowland and his chair the gold medal at the Third International Furniture Exhibition. One of the most meaningful honors for him, however, was the highly rigorous Master Design Award, which he won in 1965 from the magazine *Product Engineering*. This contest chose winners based on engineering and design merits, and that spoke to Rowland's pride in his chair as invention, not styling.

INTERNATIONAL DESIGN AWARDS

October 16, 1964

Mr. David Rowland
49 West 55th Street
New York, N. Y.

Dear Mr. Rowland:

It gives me great pleasure to inform you that you have been
selected to receive the 1965 A.I.D. International Design Award
in the Business Furniture category for your GF 40/4 Stacking
and Ganging Chair.

This Award will be presented at a gala A.I.D. International
Design Awards Dinner to be held in the Great Hall of the
Pick Congress Hotel in Chicago on Sunday evening,
January 3, 1965 at 7:00 P.M. We cordially invite you to be
our guest at the dinner to accept the Award. In the event you
will be unable to be present, please advise us immediately who
will take your place.

May I take this opportunity to compliment and congratulate you
on behalf of the National Board of Governors and members of
the American Institute of Interior Designers.

Sincerely yours,

Everett Brown, F.A.I.D.
Chairman Awards Program

AMERICAN INSTITUTE OF INTERIOR DESIGNERS • 673 FIFTH AVE. • NEW YORK 22, N.Y.

MASTER DESIGN AWARD

for achievement in product development
is presented this 19th day of May 1965
by Product Engineering to:

David Rowland

for an outstanding example of the integration of the resources
of engineering with those of design, manufacturing and marketing in the...

STACKABLE CHAIR

manufactured and introduced by:

GENERAL FIREPROOFING COMPANY

ATTESTED TO: *for* PRODUCT ENGINEERING   JUDGES:

ELMER J. TANGERMAN, editor

DR. W. W. GILBERT, General Electric Company

DONALD L. McFARLAND, Latham, Tyler, Jensen

JACOB RABINOW, Rabinow Electronics Company

RICHARD J. LeMANNA, Monroe International Corporation

F. K. POWELL JR., American Machine & Foundry Company

MARTIN A. TOLCOTT, Dunlap and Associates Inc.

RAYMOND SPILMAN, Raymond Spilman Industrial Design

↑
Master Design
Award from *Product
Engineering* magazine,
which recognized the
technical innovations
of his 40/4 Chair.

←
The American Institute
of Interior Designers
selected the 40/4 Chair
for its International
Design Award in the
Business Furniture
category, 1965.

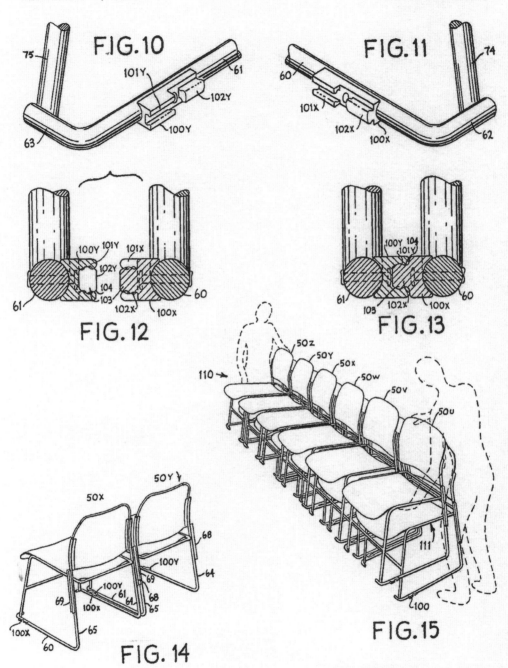

FIG.10

FIG.11

FIG.12

FIG.13

FIG.14

FIG.15

DAVID L. ROWLAND
INVENTOR.

BY

Commitment to patents

After obtaining U.S. patents in 1963, Rowland couldn't afford the $839 fees and application costs to obtain European patents. (GF didn't have the chair out on the market yet, so royalty income had not begun to flow in.) He borrowed the money at 100 percent interest to secure the European patents, a circumstance that reflects just how deeply committed he was to patenting his work.

The importance of patents had been burned into Rowland following his experience in Detroit when an auto company used one of his unprotected designs. Rowland dedicated significant resources to the process of patenting his work all through his career. He focused on obtaining utility patents, which protect the way a product is used and works, rather than design patents, which protect the way a product looks. Utility patents were and are much more difficult to get, requiring more time and money. Rowland's application for the 40/4 Chair carefully described the problems the chair solved and its unique solutions. He patented specific aspects, such as the ganging mechanism, and the rolling dolly, a separate, independent invention that allowed a stack of forty chairs to be rolled with ease. Later, he expanded the capacity of this invention to a quadruple dolly that allowed 160 chairs to be rolled with ease.

Right after the 40/4 came out, contract furniture companies set to work trying to get around Rowland's patents and come up with a competing stackable chair of their own. According to rumors, one very famous competitor spent five years and five million dollars in the attempt. But Rowland's carefully crafted patent held off competitors for years. Knockoffs have followed, but none has matched the 40/4. It is unsurpassed to this day. Every authentic 40/4 Chair has Rowland's signature under the seat.

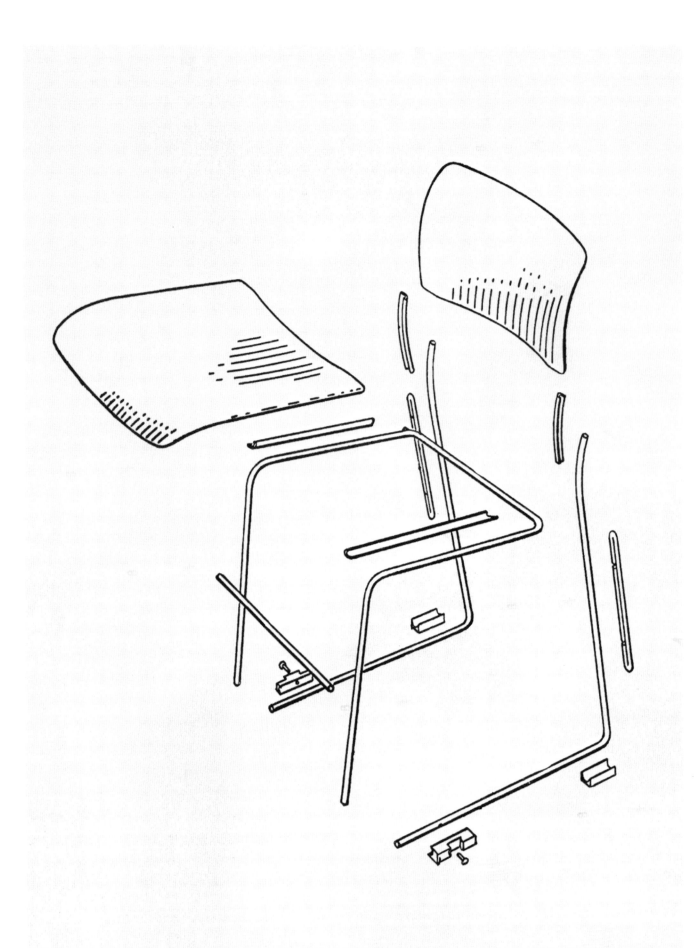

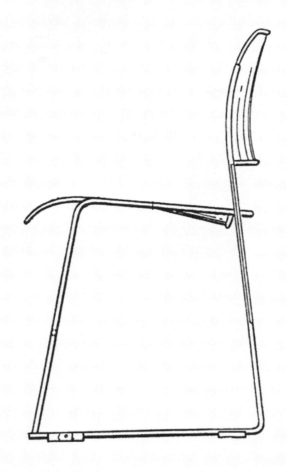

DAVID L. ROWLAND

INVENTOR.

BY

Owen, Wickersham & Erickson,

Attorneys

DAVID ROWLAND'S 40/4 CHAIR

The universal chair packed with structural innovations

David Rowland

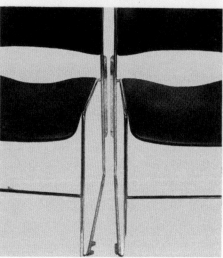

Industrial Designer David Rowland—disciple of Moholy-Nagy, Cranbrook graduate and one-time Norman Bel Geddes assistant—has designed a chair adaptable for any kind of interior or exterior use, both residential and institutional. It is also light weight, economical, maintenance-free, virtually indestructible, and stacks, gangs, and stores in amazingly little space and it is beautiful in an unassuming way, and comfortable in both upright and lounging postures. It is called the 40/4 chair, because 40 chairs stacked on a dolly stand only four feet high.

Hardly had production of the 40/4 chair been begun by the manufacturer, General Fireproofing Company, Youngstown, Ohio, when the Museum of Modern Art in New York snapped up all available models for the May 27th opening of its new galleries. The second production run was snapped up for the U.S.A. space at the Triennale of Milan this summer.

The seat and back are formed out of sheet metal coated with a heavily textured vinyl coating, Armorhide. This composite, unlike molded fiber glass, conducts heat away from the body so that the occupant remains cool and comfortable over long periods. The frame of 7/16-inch steel rod is made up of four members—two side members and two stretchers: one at front base and one at the rear of the seat. Structural reinforcements in the form of fins at rear of frames prevent base from developing side sway. These fins also *(continued on page* 135)

David Rowland: 40/4 Chair

Feature article in *Interiors* magazine, 1964. Rowland's invention received critical acclaim as soon as it was introduced.

Why the 40/4 Chair was revolutionary

Time can show whether accolades hold true. But time can also cloud perception, and when an invention is so successful that it becomes part of the built environment, adopted into wide use, it becomes invisible. We forget the original problem that was solved, and why it was needed in the first place.

Although a few stackable chairs did exist before the 40/4, they were bulky and uncomfortable, needed lots of storage space, were awkward to handle, and could not be moved about easily. Folding chairs also existed, but they took time to assemble and disassemble, their joints broke easily, and they were ugly.

The 40/4 Chair was indeed revolutionary because it made mass seating easily portable and practical, and it created possibilities that simply hadn't existed before. Two people could set up or stow away as many as 500 chairs in ten minutes. A tower of 40/4s needed a very small footprint of floor space. This meant a schoolroom of chairs could be kept in a closet. The chairs glided on and off the stack and were easy to handle. Large and small rooms could be transformed quickly for different kinds of events. In no time, a single room could become a theater. A conference room could be cleared of chairs to rapidly create a stand-up reception area.

But there are other reasons why the chair did things that no chair had done before. In an era before the term "ergonomic" was common, the 40/4 was unprecedented in its comfort for sitting over long periods, and, in addition to being beautiful and elegant, it could somehow fit perfectly anywhere. In a home, at a dining-room table, the 40/4 was so slim that it could be stacked and used, imperceptibly, in doubles. Seating for four could instantly be uncoupled to become seating for eight, should guests appear. In a large hall, when fewer seats were needed, one row of chairs ganged together could be lifted and placed on another row, making two rows magically into one.

As it broke design boundaries, the 40/4 Chair seemed to embrace paradoxes. It was deceptively simple but embodied rigorous design thinking. Its gentle, contoured lines disguised its rugged durability. It both created space and saved space. The chair could blend into an environment, or it could be bold and bright, depending on the color. It reflected many of the ideas of the mid-century era, but it transcended its time to become much bigger and more enduring.

The 40/4 created a whole new category of high-density multifunctional seating. By any measure, it was a groundbreaking design that expanded the very idea of what a chair could be and do.

The Story of a Chair

According to designer David Rowland "it is easier to design 5,000 chairs that are different than to find five that really fulfill the two basic requirements of beauty and comfort". These two qualities—and a good deal more—have been incorporated in Mr. Rowland's "40/4 Chair" just introduced by The General Fireproofing Company of Youngstown, Ohio. The chair takes its name from the fact that forty of them stack just four feet high on a specially designed dolly cart. It not only stacks with ease, it can be ganged to form rows in a matter of seconds; what's more, it can be stacked in rows of six. The slim, slender profile of the design completely belies the comfort it offers, an attribute achieved only after long testing to find the contour that would best fit the greatest number of human shapes. (Mr. Rowland admits to using his friends as guinea pigs). The frame of the chair consists of only four elements of strong steel rod. The subtly contoured metal seat and back panels are coated in a vinyl finish which closely resembles the look and texture of leather. Designed for use in auditoriums, lecture rooms and other areas which require mass seating, the "40/4 Chair" makes its first big public appearance in the new building of the Museum of Modern Art which opened on May 25th. It has also been accepted for exhibition at the 13th Triennale di Milano. In designing the chair, Mr. Rowland set two goals for himself: to develop the most universally useful chair ever made and to accomplish it with the least expenditure of materials and labor. He has admirably succeeded.

V.I.P.*

Stacks Up in a New Way

This firm's new 40/4 chair, designed by David Rowland, solves some pressing problems for mass seating centers. It fills requirements of comfort, space, storage and ease of handling, while retaining a tasteful appearance. As the title 40/4 implies, 40 chairs can be stacked in four feet and they may be furnished with ganging or joining principle. A room may be completely furnished with the chairs in mere minutes. The over-all requirement of sitting comfort for people of all sizes for any length of time has also been fulfilled, according to the manufacturer. For instance, almost imperceptible bulges on each side of the lower curve of the back panel give just the support one needs for the small of the back. This functional stacking chair which combines strength with lightness of weight is available in two finishes: chrome plated or with vinyl coated leg members. The General Fireproofing Co., IM, Youngstown, Ohio. Circle 300 on page 155.

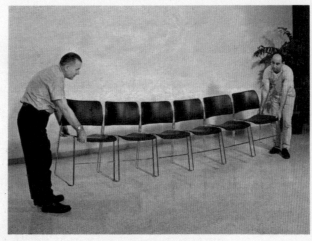 

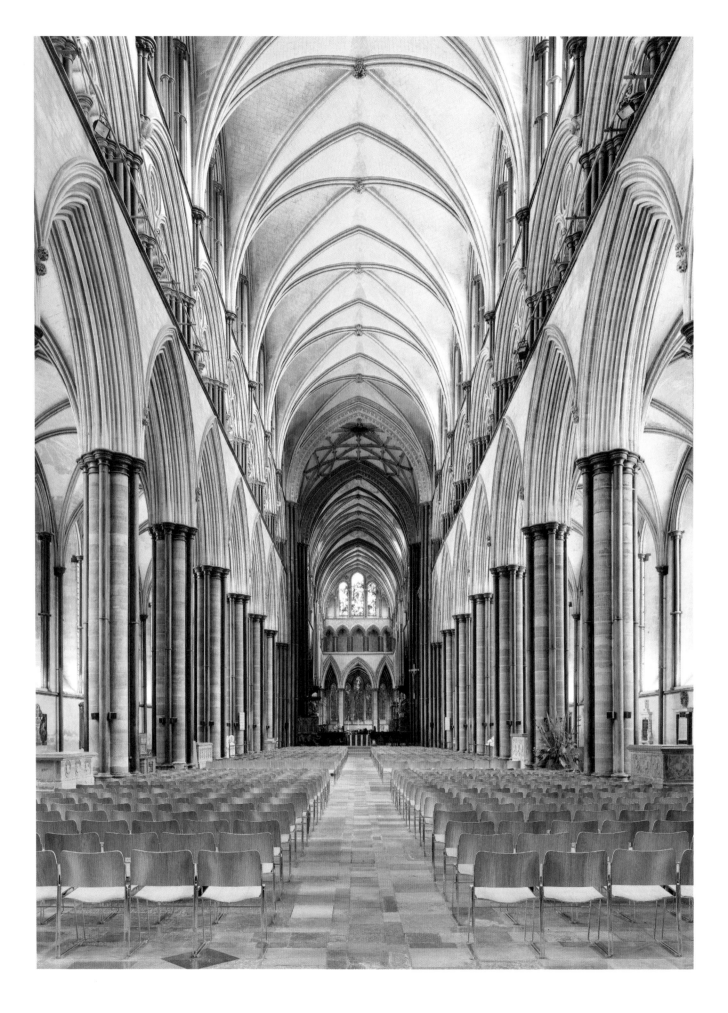

David Rowland: 40/4 Chair

Oak veneer 40/4 Chairs
fit seamlessly in the
early English Gothic
architecture of the
beautiful Salisbury
Cathedral, UK, built in
the thirteenth century.

Critical response and multimillions sold

"To say that this chair has influenced subsequent designs would be a gross understatement ... No other design has yet achieved the beautiful simplicity and total appropriateness of Rowland's chair."

Clement Meadmore, *The Modern Chair: Classic Designs by Thonet, Breuer, Le Corbusier, Eames and Others*, 1974

As soon as the 40/4 Chair won the Grand Prix at the Milan Triennale, orders poured in to GF. Designers, architects, and furniture dealers from around the world wanted the chair, overwhelming the firm. Despite running two shifts a day at the Forest City plant, GF was unable to keep up with demand. In a letter to a furniture-dealer friend in November 1964, Rowland described "order backlogs of several thousand." The design world that had previously rejected him could not help but take note. In the 1970s, at a cocktail party in New York, George Nelson came rushing over to Rowland, his face lit up with excitement. He threw his arm in an arc over his head and exclaimed, "When your chair hit the market, it was like a rocket shooting across the sky!"

Rowland's 40/4 Chair is housed in the permanent collections of some of the world's greatest museums, including MoMA and the Metropolitan Museum of Art in New York; the Art Institute of Chicago; the National Gallery and British Museum in London; Copenhagen's Design Museum; and the Centre Pompidou and Musée d'Orsay in Paris. In 2016, the Art Institute of Chicago chose the 40/4 as one of twelve great modern chairs, alongside those designed by Ray and Charles Eames, Harry Bertoia, Alvar Aalto, Eero Saarinen, Ludwig Mies van der Rohe, and Le Corbusier, among others. The 40/4 has been installed in some of the most iconic places including the world-famous St. Paul's Cathedral in London, which, in the 1970s, replaced its old seating with 3,500 40/4 Chairs. The chairs have been in daily use ever since and have also seated guests at important events such as Prince Charles and Lady Diana Spencer's wedding in 1981 and Queen Elizabeth's Platinum Jubilee in 2022.

By the first years of the twenty-first century, eight million 40/4 Chairs had been sold, and counting stopped. They are now to be seen in every conceivable venue, in cultural, corporate, educational, worship, and public spaces everywhere. In 2017, *Architectural Digest* included the 40/4 Chair in its list of the most successful product designs in history. In her book *100 Midcentury Chairs and Their Stories* (2016), the design writer Lucy Ryder Richardson described the 40/4 as "still the go-to stacking chair for large interior events, museums, and cultural centers around the world. Unsurpassed in terms of engineering. Ergonomically correct and beautiful to look at from every angle."

David Rowland: 40/4 Chair

↑
40/4 Chairs in the
Scottish Parliament,
Edinburgh.

←

A sea of blue 40/4
Chairs, Essec Business
School, Cergy, France.

Red 40/4 Chairs in the
grand setting of the
main hall in Copenhagen
City Hall, Denmark.

David Rowland: 40/4 Chair

　　　　　　　　　　　　　David Rowland: 40/4 Chair

↑
Black stained veneer
40/4 Chairs at the Ny
Carlsberg Glyptotek art
museum in Copenhagen,
Denmark.

←
Wood veneer 40/4
Chairs at the
Biblioteca Central
de la UNED, a major
university library in
Madrid, Spain.

↑
Bright and contemporary
multicolored 40/4
Chairs with white
powder-coated frames
in the Biblioteca
Movimente Chivasso,
a library in
Chivasso, Italy.

David Rowland: 40/4 Chair

↓
The elegant minimal
design of the 40/4
Chair lends itself
to the streamlined
contemporary design
of the First Church
of Christ, Scientist,
Washington, D.C., USA.

Overleaf:
40/4 Chairs fill
contrasting worship
spaces around the
world, from grand
cathedrals to this
quiet naturalistic
setting, with warm
wood and a view of
trees just outside
the window, Unitarian
Universalist Fellowship
of Central Oregon,
Bend, Oregon, USA.

The 40/4 Chair: A Story of Persistence and Revolutionary Design

→
The simplicity of
the black 40/4 Chairs
against the fresh
white walls creates
a stunning performance
space at Mogens
Dahl Concert Hall,
Copenhagen, Denmark.

Overleaf:
40/4 Chairs in veneer
were chosen for
Kasarmikatu 21, a
multipurpose workspace
with platinum-level
LEED environmental
rating, serving a
thousand employees
in Helsinki Finland.

David Rowland: 40/4 Chair

David Rowland: 40/4 Chair

↑
The 40/4 in red amid
towering pink brick
walls at the Biblioteca
Umanistica dei
Paolotti, University
of Parma, Italy.

←
In orange, green, and
pink. The versatility
of the 40/4 Chair
lends itself to the
contemporary structure
of the Tenerife School
of Scenic Arts, Canary
Islands, Spain.

Overleaf:
A ring of 40/4 Chairs,
Caermersklooster,
originally a Carmelite
monastery and church
built in the Middle
Ages, now a center
for the arts in Ghent,
Belgium.

Selling globally

GF was not set up as an international organization. As orders and interest in the 40/4 Chair poured in from around the world, the company opened an office in Brussels to meet demand. However, by the early 1980s, the firm wanted to get out of the international business and sold its European licensing rights to the 40/4 Chair to HOWE a/s, a furniture company founded in Connecticut in 1928, now headquartered in Denmark. It was an ideal match. HOWE specialized in versatile and multifunctional furniture, with simple, Bauhaus-inspired designs. Under its leadership, the 40/4 Chair grew and deepened its presence all over Europe and in other world markets.

GF held North American rights until 1989, when—with so many other American manufacturers of the era—it sold its assets and closed its doors. A large, diversified holding company named Tang Industries bought GF and continued to sell and manufacture the 40/4 Chair through its subsidiaries in North America. A new era arrived when HOWE bought the U.S. and Canadian rights to the 40/4 Chair in 2013. Since then, HOWE has been the leading manufacturer of the 40/4 Chair.

Versatility

Because of its timelessness and versatility, the 40/4 Chair continues to be specified in the most diverse architectural settings possible. In a library in Parma, Italy, the 40/4 appears in vibrant red amid bright white tables. In an educational space in the Canary Islands, a white meeting table is arranged with pink, green, and orange 40/4 Chairs. At the British Antarctic Survey's futuristic Halley VI Research Station on the Brunt Ice Shelf, the 40/4 Chair maximizes very limited space at a table where the staff gather. In the medieval Canterbury Cathedral in southern England, the 40/4 is set up and cleared away quickly to transform the space from seated to standing events.

It is amazing to consider the vast impact of the 40/4 Chair. What started out as a tiny spark of an idea on a hot Sunday afternoon in New York City has grown to benefit countless millions of people, including many we might not even think of, from all those who were employed to build, produce, market, and sell the chair over the decades, to those many people whose work was made easier by being able to set up and break down gathering spaces with efficiency and ease. The chair has provided comfort to people around the globe who have sat in it for long periods, whether during worship or classes or conferences or events. Finally, fusing the useful with the sublime, the chair has given us a timeless exemplar of comfort, efficiency, economy, and craft, and in doing so it has inspired generations of designers to innovate and create new seating of their own.

Continuing to Design: New York, The World, Virginia

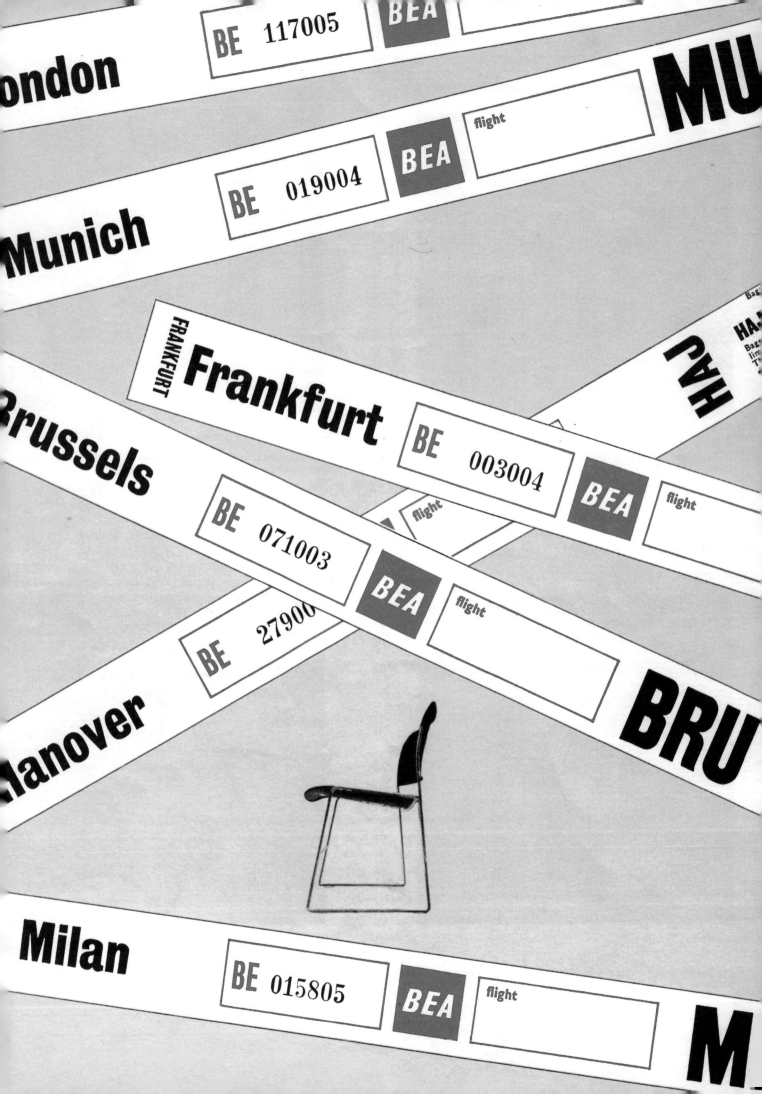

Page from General
Fireproofing
Company newsletter,
1968, celebrating
the "Triumphant
European Tour" of
the 40/4 Chair.

The success of the 40/4 Chair ushered in a new chapter in Rowland's career and life. In response to interest from architects and designers outside the United States, he went on an extensive tour of Europe, working with GF, which held receptions in London, Munich, Frankfurt, Hamburg, Brussels, Hanover, Milan, Vienna, and Paris. He was also in demand as a speaker all over the USA, invited to address audiences at design and architecture conferences in New York, Chicago, San Francisco, Los Angeles, Dallas, Washington, D.C., and more. In 1968, he addressed an audience of several thousand at the Smithsonian Museum in conjunction with its exhibition *Please Be Seated*, which covered the evolution of seating over 4,000 years. The 40/4 Chair was selected to be one of seventy-four chairs featured in the show, which then traveled around the country.

In New York, Rowland rented his own office space on the ground floor of a beautiful Beaux Arts building at 8 East 62nd Street, only steps from Central Park. He had two rooms, big enough for several drawing boards and a couple of desks, and there was a little garden out back. He never expanded his firm to take on other industrial designers, although he did have a small staff, including a secretary and an assistant. The most important of these was Malcolm Peach, a trained designer from the United Kingdom who specialized in furniture. Peach had come to the USA in 1966 and shortly afterward went to work for Rowland, staying with him for seventeen years.

Rowland continued to rent tools and workspace by the hour until about 1970, when he got his own workshop in addition to his office. Like many New York City artists and creative people of the time, he was attracted to the largely empty warehouses and factories of the SoHo neighborhood in downtown Manhattan, where ironclad buildings offered vast loft space with tall ceilings, large windows, and inexpensive rents. Rowland took the entire second floor of 462 Broome Street, where he set up tools and machines to embark freely on experimentation and prototype development of his many ideas.

While Rowland didn't hesitate to buy the new materials he needed, he also looked for new ways of using those that already existed. He enjoyed going to junkyards to find cast-off or intriguing items that he could use. His workshop in SoHo lent itself to similar pursuits. It was just two blocks from Canal Street, which was notorious for its row of hawkers and shops offering all manner of odd goods out on the sidewalks, from hardware and construction supplies to electronics and clothing. He liked to go there and rummage among the baskets and barrels for something he could explore or use.

After he had been more than a dozen years on Broome Street, SoHo was becoming increasingly fashionable, and Rowland's landlord quadrupled his rent. He left that building and established a studio at 523 East 72nd Street, bringing his business office there from East 62nd Street as well. His new location was a large building near the East River, filled with craftspeople, including leathersmiths, gilders, upholsterers, and furniture-makers. After only a few years, when that building was sold and turned into co-ops, he (and many others from this location) moved operations to a building at 315 East 91st Street, also filled with craftspeople.

David Rowland: 40/4 Chair

←
Rowland delivering a
talk titled "The Moral
Basis of Design" to a
crowd of 3,000 at the
Smithsonian Institute,
Washington, D.C.

↓
The 40/4 Chair was
included in the
Please be Seated
exhibition at the
Cooper-Hewitt,
Smithsonian Design
Museum in conjunction
with the Decorative
Arts Program of the
American Federation
of Arts.

PLEASE BE SEATED

THE AMERICAN FEDERATION OF ARTS

Erwin Wassum Rowland
with David Rowland in
front of the Guggenheim
Museum. Kindred
spirits, they were
married in 1971.

Marriage

In the fall of 1968, at a party held by some mutual church friends, Rowland met the woman who would become his wife: Erwin Wassum, a Virginian who had worked at the Museum of Modern Art in New York. Rowland had noticed her there on many occasions, but by the time they met, she'd left the museum to pursue her own interest in art and design. They began seeing each other.

Erwin lived in a converted townhouse on East 72nd Street in Manhattan, in a one-bedroom apartment with little floor space but very high ceilings. One Tuesday evening, not long after she and Rowland had begun dating, they were at a restaurant together, when she bemoaned the fact that she didn't have room in her small apartment for a studio. Rowland, ever ready to solve a design challenge, suggested that the ceilings were so high, there was space to build a loft in her bedroom to create a workroom. She said it was a great idea, but she didn't know anyone who could build it. Rowland answered that it would be very simple to do, and he would do it. He drew out a plan on a napkin and said he would come over the next day, Wednesday, to measure, then order the lumber on Thursday, have it delivered on Friday, and build it on Saturday. All this he did, to her delight. There was just one thing missing, which was a way to get up to the loft. Rowland suggested a ladder, but Erwin wanted stairs. So, he came over again and measured for stairs, which he built for her the following weekend.

Rowland and Erwin shared a love of art and design in addition to many other interests. They dated frequently. But Rowland was not one to rush into marriage, and it was not until June 1971 that they became husband and wife.

The couple lived on East 73rd Street for the next thirty years. In 1976, they also bought a property with four old farm buildings near the ocean in Bridgehampton, Long Island. They worked weekends with a carpenter and his helper for more than a year to turn two of the buildings into a house. Rowland designed and drew up the plans, while Erwin was the general contractor. Both enjoyed all the hands-on work. The place was their getaway and retreat, as well as a gathering place for family and friends, for the next twenty-nine years.

David Rowland: 40/4 Chair

Immediately after the
release of the 40/4
Chair, Rowland began
developing variations
of it with additional
functions and finishes.

←
The 40/4 Chair in
wood veneer.

↓
A 40/4 armchair,
side chair, and chair
with tablet and book
storage rack.

New designs and inventions

Expanding the 40/4 into a family of chairs
Immediately after the release of the 40/4 Chair, Rowland began working on additions and variations to his award-winning design. One of the first was a flip-up writing tablet that could be attached to the chair, and he also designed an armchair. In addition, he worked with GF on new variations of materials, such as molded veneer and upholstery for the seats and backs.

174 David Rowland: 40/4 Chair

Prototype for the
Take Home Sofa, 1969.
Rowland designed and
patented a completely
collapsible sofa that
could be flat-packed
in a box.

Despite its groovy
period packaging, the
collapsible sofa was
way ahead of its time,
preceding the enormous
flat-packed furniture
business that arrived
decades later.

Flat-packed sofa

In the 1960s, when sofa-buying meant going to a store, placing an order, and waiting weeks or months to receive delivery on a truck, Rowland designed a slim-profile collapsible sofa that could be purchased on the spot, put in a box (with the customer's choice of cushion covers), rolled out of the store on wheels, put in the car, taken home, unfolded, and set up—all in a morning. He obtained patents on his sofa, which included forty-four claims and eighty-six drawings, but he did not find a manufacturer for the Take Home Sofa (a product that has now taken over the market in today's vast online "sofa in a box" business). Nonetheless, he kept it on the back burner. In the 1980s he returned to the idea, redesigned it, and succeeded in licensing it to Martela of Finland.

David Rowland: 40/4 Chair

↑
Light enough to be
transported with ease
by one person up a
flight of stairs.

←
A model demonstrates
that the Take Home
Sofa is so compact
that it can fit in
a Volkswagen Bug.

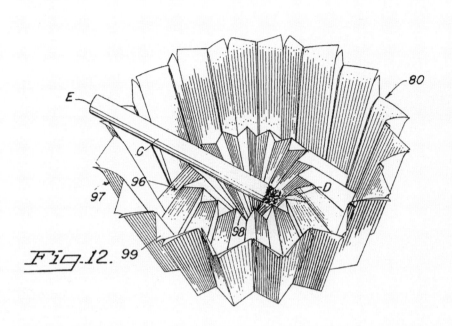

Fig.12.

Fig.14.

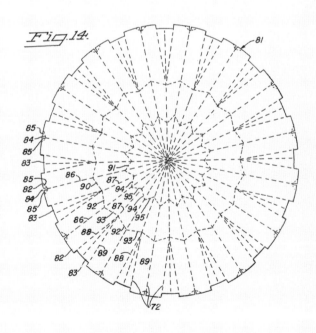

Disposable Safety
Ashtray, 1967. Rowland
did not smoke himself
but saw a need for
a safer ashtray to
prevent the many fatal
fires and damage caused
by lit cigarettes.

Rowland's patented
design ensured that
cigarettes always fell
into the ashtray and
not out. They were
made of a disposable
fireproof material that
could be discarded
after use, especially
in restaurants,
assuring a clean table
for the next diners.

Fire-prevention and disposable safety ashtray

When he became aware of the high number of fires, injuries, damage, and deaths caused by cigarette smoking, Rowland, who was not a smoker himself, became interested in and researched the problem. In 1967, he designed a safer ashtray, made with two concentric and stackable cup-shaped receptacles, configured to ensure that cigarettes fell into the trays, rather than out. He used a disposable fireproof material, such as nonflammable metal-foil-backed paper. The ashtrays came in stacks, and the topmost ashtray could be lifted off easily once used, leaving a clean one underneath, an especially useful feature for the hospitality industry at a time when smoking was still permitted in restaurants. Although the invention never made it to market, it reflects his dedication to problem-solving designs and boundaryless thinking that allowed him to go beyond chairs. Rowland patented his ashtray, too.

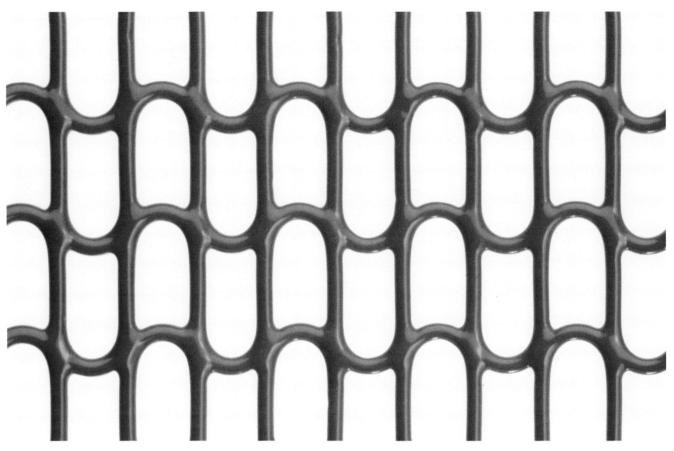

David Rowland: 40/4 Chair

Always searching for
comfort without bulk,
Rowland invented Soflex,
a new seating material
made of arcuate sinuous
springs coated in vinyl
plastisol. The result
was a thin, resilient,
and soft seat.

The Softec Chair,
1979. Rowland
incorporated Soflex
into his new compactly
stackable chair.

Soflex: A new seating material

In 1973, Rowland returned to his interest in arcuate sinuous springs, which had fascinated him since his days at Cranbrook. He invented a new material that he called Soflex, made of the sinuous metal springs dipped in vinyl plastisol. When cured, the plastisol hardened and held the springs together, forming a resilient open-mesh material that could be applied to unique seat frames. Previously, if designers wanted a thin seating material, they had to rely on something hard, such as plastic or molded plywood, and if they wanted something soft, it had to be thick and unwieldy, such as foam cushioning. Soflex solved this predicament, affording a thin, extremely comfortable seat. Rowland saw endless opportunities for it in seating applications as wide-ranging as buses, planes, tractors, and stadiums.

However, getting the material to be made perfectly was a major undertaking that took years of development. First, it was necessary for Rowland to find the right springs, with steel of the right gauge that could be made consistently with precision. Then there was the development of the right plastisol solution and production technique, and a machine to implement the manufacturing process. Working with a small company in Connecticut, Rowland and Peach spent many months traveling to the factory, conducting experiments in plastisol solutions and dipping methods, to perfect the process.

The Softec Chair

Rowland incorporated his Soflex material into the design of two important chairs. The first he called the Softec Chair. It was made of 7/8 in (2.2 cm) diameter 14-gauge tubular-steel frames, with seats and backs made of Soflex in six color options. The chairs could be stacked, freestanding or on a dolly, and came in numerous variations: side chair, armchair, bar chair, outdoor chair, tablet chair, and children's chair. Rowland licensed the Softec Chair to Thonet USA, which manufactured it. In 1979, it was introduced at NeoCon, the leading design conference in the United States. The chair won two Institute of Business Designers Gold Medals.

Over the years, Rowland continued his friendship with Bucky Fuller, maintaining an ongoing conversation about purpose-driven design. (Whenever they could, the Rowlands attended Fuller's lectures around the northeastern USA.) While he was working on the Softec Chair, Rowland heard that Fuller would be speaking at Hunter College in Manhattan and staying in a nearby hotel. He set up a meeting to show Fuller his Softec Chair. The chair's design, materials, and concept reflected many of the ideas that the two men had discussed over the years—especially the development of the Soflex material itself. When Rowland showed Fuller the chair at the meeting, his response was, "Brilliant. Where can I get some?" It was a great moment of validation for Rowland, who later sent Fuller two of the chairs as a gift.

[11] 3,767,261

[45] Oct. 23, 1973

[54] **SEATING AND SUB-ASSEMBLY FOR SEATS AND BACKS AND METHOD FOR MAKING SAME**

[76] Inventor: **David L. Rowland,** 8 E. 62nd St., New York, N.Y. 10021

[22] Filed: **Mar. 22, 1971**

[21] Appl. No.: **126,563**

[52] U.S. Cl...................... **297/452,** 5/309, 297/239, 297/445
[51] Int. Cl............................. **A47c 3/04,** A47c 7/14
[58] Field of Search.................... 297/239, 445, 450, 297/452, 454, 458; 160/386–404; 117/99, 178, 128.7, 133; 5/309, 354; 267/111, 44, 109; 161/112, 118

[56]   **References Cited**

UNITED STATES PATENTS

2,803,293	8/1957	Rowland	297/445 UX
3,404,916	10/1968	Rowland	297/239
2,731,076	1/1956	Rowland	297/452 UX
3,082,438	3/1963	Nachman, Jr.	5/353

Primary Examiner—Casmir A. Nunberg
Attorney—Owen, Wickersham & Erickson

[57]   **ABSTRACT**

Seats and backs for chairs and other seating units are made as a sub-assembly of sinuous spring wires. Each wire touches its adjacent wire at least once per cycle, and each of the wires extends when in the sub-assembly and before placed therein as a cylindrical arc, so that the assembly itself is a cylindrical arc. A thin sleeve-like plastic coating surrounds the wires and follows their sinuous shapes, linking the wires together wherever they touch or closely approach each other, to provide the unitary assembly. In fact, the assembly is held together solely by this plastic coating. The assembly is intended to be flattened somewhat when installed on a chair frame, to place the springs in tension along a flatter cylindrical arc, and this tension is one of the main forces retaining the wires in place. The assembly, whether coated or not, is mounted at or near the ends of the individual wires on a suitable securing member of the frame. In preferred forms of the invention the plastic coating has an A scale Shore durometer between 45 and 90, so that the assembly is held together by the plastic coating without substantially restraining the flexing of the spring wires, while the coating also provides a spring action itself between the adjacent wires, by stretching and contracting, giving a two-way stretch. Front and rear border wires may be added to the assembly if desired and held to the adjacent sinuous wires by the plastic coating. A method for making such a sub-assembly is shown, as is a method for installing a sub-assembly on a suitable frame.

32 Claims, 39 Drawing Figures

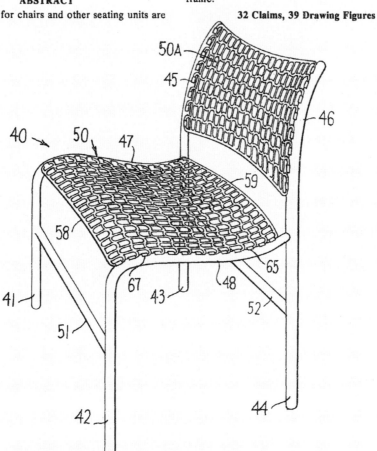

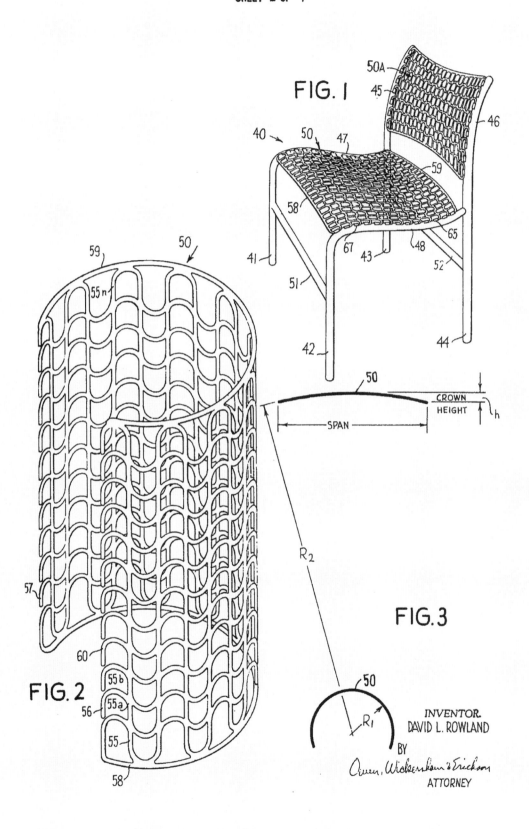

FIG. I

FIG. 2

FIG.3

INVENTOR.
DAVID L. ROWLAND

BY

Owen, Wickersham & Erichson

ATTORNEY

A Gralla Publication

NOVEMBER 1979

Contract

THE BUSINESS MAGAZINE OF COMMERCIAL FURNISHINGS & INTERIOR ARCHITECTURE

IBD/ CONTRACT PRODUCT DESIGN AWARD WINNERS

Sof-Tech seating wins Thonet top gold award

Shearman & Sterling private offices are systems furniture

Gensler & Associates facilities guide sets office standards

V.A.'s own offices designed to meet needs of handicapped

EXECUTIVE BUYER EDITION

BONUS CIRCULATION: 5,000 OFFICE MANAGERS & FACILITY PLANNING EXECUTIVES

←
Rowland licensed the
Softec Chair to Thonet
USA and introduced it
at the NeoCon design
conference in Chicago,
1979. The chair came
with an upholstery
sleeve option to cover
the springs.

↑
Rowland with his Softec
Chair, which won two
Institute of Business
Designers Gold Medals.

Sinuous Stackers from Thonet

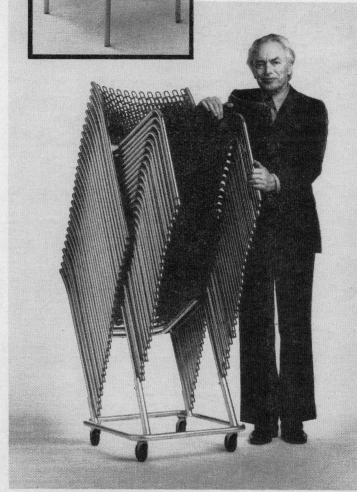

David Rowland and Thonet's Sof-Tech stack chair

David Rowland has an answer for everone who ever complained about too-soft seating: sit on springs. He has the same answer for people who complain about traditional stack chairs. Sof-Tech, the stacking chair Rowland designed for Thonet, is a network of coated sinuous springs and a 14 gauge tubular steel frame. If you don't think of a sinuous spring as sculpture (David Rowland does) you can do on-the-spot upholstery with a pair of padded zippered sleeves in vinyl of Sierra fabric. Ganging connectors are optional, as are nylon glides and stacking bumpers. A stack 30 chairs high is only 5'5". Thonet, P.O. Box 1587, York, PA 17405.□

Circle 43

← A stack of thirty Softec Chairs fit in a space 5 ft 6 in tall.

→ A *New York Times* article described the Softec Chair as "technologically advanced."

New Seating: Revivals And Innovations

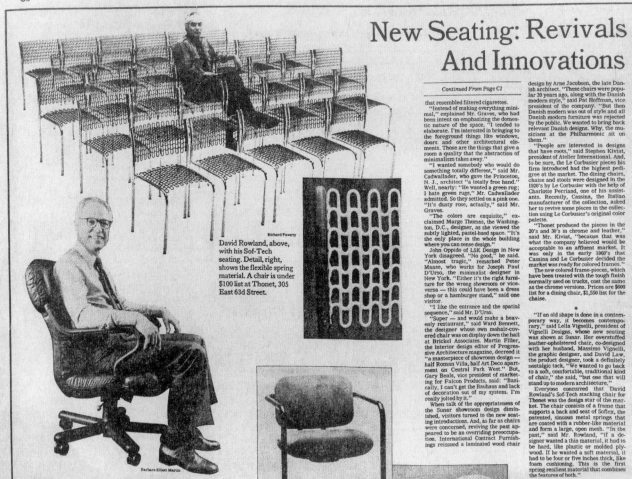

Richard Faverty

David Rowland, above, with his Sof-Tech seating. Detail, right, shows the flexible spring material. A chair is under $100 list at Thonet, 305 East 63d Street.

Barbara Elliott Martin

Continued From Page C1

that resembled filtered cigarettes.

"Instead of making everything minimal," explained Mr. Graves, who had been intent on emphasizing the domestic nature of the space, "I tended to elaborate. I'm interested in bringing to the foreground things like windows, doors and other architectural elements. Those are the things that give a room a quality that the abstraction of minimalism takes away."

"I wanted somebody who would do something totally different," said Mr. Cadwallader, who gave the Princeton, N. J., architect "a totally free hand." Well, nearly: "He wanted a green rug; I hate green rugs," Mr. Cadwallader admitted. So they settled on a pink one. "It's dusty rose, actually," said Mr. Graves.

"The colors are exquisite," exclaimed Marge Thomas, the Washington, D.C., designer, as she viewed the subtly lighted, pastel-hued space. "It's the only place in the whole building where you can sense design."

John Oppido of LSK Design in New York disagreed. "No good," he said. "Almost tragic," remarked Peter Maase, who works for Joseph Paul D'Urso, the minimalist designer in New York. "Either it's the right furniture for the wrong showroom or vice-versa — this could have been a dress shop or a hamburger stand," said one visitor.

"I like the entrance and the spatial sequence," said Mr. D'Urso.

"Super — and would make a heavenly restaurant," said Ward Bennett, the designer whose own mohair-covered chair was on display down the hall at Brickel Associates. Martin Filler, the interior design editor of Progressive Architecture magazine, decreed it "a masterpiece of showroom design — half Roman Villa, half Art Deco apartment on Central Park West." But, Gary Beals, vice president of marketing for Falcon Products, said: "Basically, I can't get the Bauhaus and lack of decoration out of my system. I'm really jolted by it."

When talk of the appropriateness of the Sunar showroom design diminished, visitors turned to the new seating introductions. And, as far as chairs were concerned, reviving the past appeared to be an overriding preoccupation. International Contract Furnishings reissued a laminated wood chair

design by Arne Jacobsen, the late Danish architect. "These chairs were popular 20 years ago, along with the Danish modern style," said Pat Hoffman, vice president of the company. "But then Danish modern was out of style and all Danish modern furniture was rejected by the public. We wanted to bring back relevant Danish designs. Why, the musicians at the Philharmonic sit on them."

"People are interested in designs that have roots," said Stephen Kiviat, president of Atelier International. And, to be sure, the Le Corbusier pieces his firm introduced had the highest pedigree at the market. The dining chairs, chaise and stools were designed in the 1920's by Le Corbusier with the help of Charlotte Perriand, one of his assistants. Recently, Cassina, the Italian manufacturer of the collection, asked her to revive some pieces in the collection using Le Corbusier's original color palette.

"Thonet produced the pieces in the 20's and 30's in chrome and leather," said Mr. Kiviat, "because that was what the company believed would be acceptable to an affluent market. It was only in the early 1960's that Cassina and Le Corbusier decided the market was ready for colored frames."

The new colored frame-pieces, which have been treated with the tough finish normally used on trucks, cost the same as the chrome versions. Prices are $600 list for a dining chair, $1,550 list for the chaise.

•

"If an old shape is done in a contemporary way, it becomes contemporary," said Lella Vignelli, president of Vignelli Designs, whose new seating was shown at Sunar. Her overstuffed leather-upholstered chair, co-designed with her husband, Massimo Vignelli, the graphic designer, and David Law, the product designer, took a definitely nostalgic tack. "We wanted to go back to a soft, comfortable, traditional kind of chair," she said, "but one that will stand up to modern architecture."

Everyone concurred that David Rowland's Sof-Tech stacking chair for Thonet was the design star of the market. The chair consists of a frame that supports a back and seat of Soflex, the patented, sinuous metal springs that are coated with a rubber-like material and form a large, open mesh. "In the past," said Mr. Rowland, "if a designer wanted a thin material, it had to be hard, like plastic or molded plywood. If he wanted a soft material, it had to be four or five inches thick, like foam cushioning. This is the first spring resilient material that combines the features of both."

David Rowland: 40/4 Chair

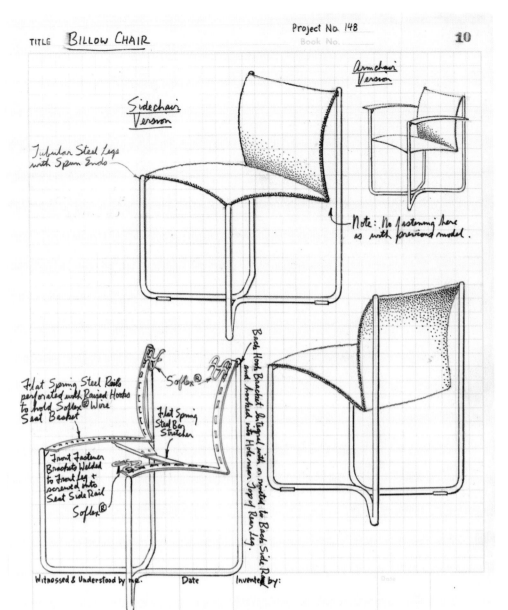

Drawings of Rowland's
Billow Chair, which
incorporated Soflex
material covered
with fabric, with
armchair and side
chair versions.

TITLE **BILLOW CHAIR**

Project No. 148

Book No.

10

Sidechair
Version

Armchair
Version

Tubular Steel Legs
with Spun Ends

Note: No fastening here
as with previous model.

Flat Spring Steel Rails
perforated with Raised Hooks
to hold Soflex® Wire
Seat Basket

Soflex®

Back Hook Bracket Bstiged with a register to Back Side Rail
and hooked into Hole near Top of Rear Leg.

Flat Spring
Steel Bar
Stretcher

Front Fastener
Brackets Welded
to Front Leg +
screwed into
Seat Side Rail

Soflex®

Witnessed & Understood by me.   Date   Invented by: Date

The Billow Chair

In 1984, Rowland came out with his Billow Chair, also built with Soflex, but this time covered with fabric. Soflex allowed the chair to have a flexible seat and back with a light, thin profile. The seat and back seemed to "float," while the lumbar curve of the chair back and the sloped edge of the seat worked together to create a snug yet relaxed, comfortable body. The chair was a minimalist icon of passive ergonomics in that it "passively," or automatically, adjusted its shape based on the natural movements of the occupant. It was manufactured by Nienkämper of Canada and won a Resources Council Product Design Award in 1989.

The Billow Chair seat and back seem to "float." The lumbar curve of the back and the sloped edge of its seat work together to create a comfortable chair. Rowland designed the Billow Chair with passive ergonomics. It is "passively," or automatically, adjusted based on the natural movements of the sitter.

David Rowland: 40/4 Chair

Modulus seating system
The Modulus system of sofas and chairs was inspired by the Take Home Sofa Rowland had designed in the 1960s. It had the same lines and easily assembled flat-pack design. This versatile, adaptable system included chairs, settees, sofas, end tables, and connecting pieces, to accommodate a large range of seating configurations. Modulus was ideal for education, hospitality, business, and residential seating. Rowland licensed it to Martela of Finland, which introduced it in 1982.

The Modulus Seating System grew out of Rowland's 1966 Take Home Sofa. Martela of Finland manufactured it.

Rowland's flat-packed system included chairs, settees, sofas, end tables, and connecting pieces that allowed a wide range of configurations.

Overleaf:
Modulus patent drawings. Modulus could be carried by one person and assembled without tools. The upholstery could be removed for easy cleaning or change.

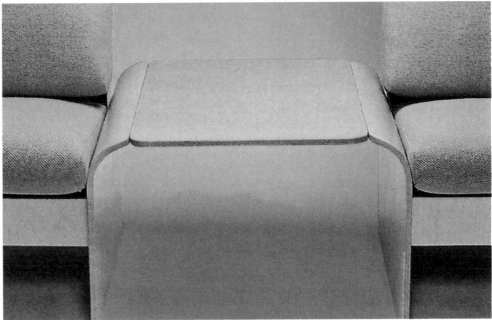

United States Patent

Rowland

[15] **3,700,282**

[45] **Oct. 24, 1972**

[54] **SEATING UNIT**

[72] Inventor: **David L. Rowland,** 49 West 55th Street, New York, N.Y. 10019

[22] Filed: **Dec. 30, 1969**

[21] Appl. No.: **889,155**

[52] **U.S. Cl.** **297/440,** 297/219, 297/416, 297/419, 297/443, 297/454
[51] **Int. Cl.**..............................**A47c 4/02,** A47c 7/54
[58] **Field of Search** ..312/257, 258, 262, 263; 5/341, 5/345, 354, 355, 356, 361; 297/218, 219, 416, 440–445, 452, 454–456

[56] **References Cited**

UNITED STATES PATENTS

659,251	10/1900	Nerad	297/218
1,174,846	3/1916	Garland	312/258 X
1,885,109	11/1932	Burkart	297/219 X
2,086,640	7/1937	Reynolds	297/218
2,439,322	4/1948	Thaden	297/440 X
2,678,088	5/1954	Jamison, Jr.	297/416
2,805,428	9/1957	Buchman	5/341
2,990,010	6/1961	Lincoln	297/440 X
3,028,279	4/1962	Heberlein	161/75
3,107,944	10/1963	Baermann	297/452
3,148,389	9/1964	Lustig	5/341
3,357,030	12/1967	George	5/357
3,363,270	1/1968	McClive	5/355
3,467,433	9/1969	Lindau et al.	297/445 X
3,515,430	6/1970	Nelson	297/219

FOREIGN PATENTS OR APPLICATIONS

1,805,650	6/1969	Germany	312/258
881,875	11/1961	Great Britain	297/218

Primary Examiner—Casmit A. Nunberg
Attorney—Owen, Wickersham & Erickson

[57] **ABSTRACT**

A seating unit, made up of: (1) a pair of side panel members, each comprising a planar vertical portion having a lower unit-supporting edge, often with a horizontal arm portion at its upper end, (2) a generally horizontal seat frame member, (3) a generally vertical back frame member having a generally vertical panel portion, often with a horizontal portion at its upper end, (4) releasable clamp or threaded means or other locking means securing each side panel member to the seat frame, (5) hinges securing the seat frame and back frame together, so that they can be folded together or erected at approximately a right angle, (6) releasable clamp or threaded means or other locking means securing the back frame to each side panel, and (7) at least one cushion with seat and back portions resting on the seat frame and back frame, the seat and back frames each being a single cushion wide or a width equal to an integral number of cushions. The unit may also have removable upholstery; this may comprise a casing of stretchable upholstery fabric with padding at least five times as thick as the fabric adhered to the fabric; a suitable undersize casing is secured releasably around each side panel and held in tension thereon, and a similar casing is held in tension on the back frame. There are numerous important structural features in the various elements.

44 Claims, 86 Drawing Figures

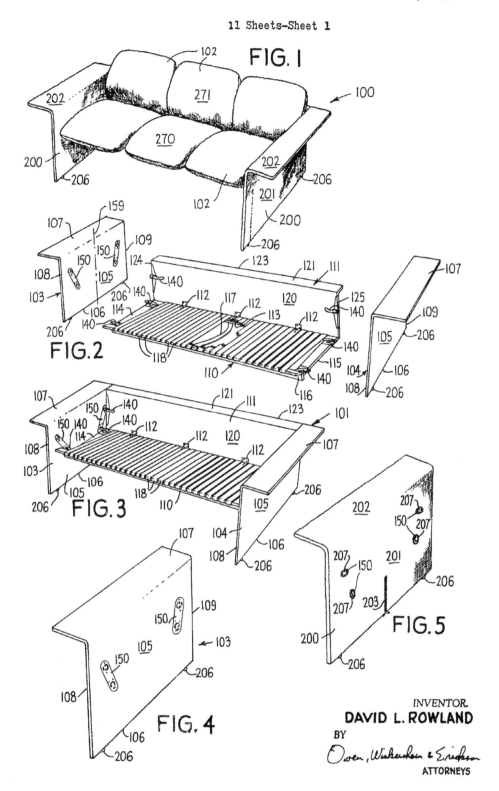

FIG. I

FIG.2

FIG.3

FIG. 4

FIG.5

INVENTOR.
DAVID L. ROWLAND
BY

Owen, Wickersham & Erickson

ATTORNEYS

Other projects: The Earl Rowland Foundation

In 1968, Rowland established a non-profit foundation to honor his father's life and career as a museum director. The Earl Rowland Foundation set out to create a library of narrated documentaries that captured significant art exhibitions at major museums in New York City. The purpose was to extend the reach and impact of exhibitions, which took months or years to assemble but were on view only for a short time. Rowland hired a veteran writer, Louis Chapin, to be the director, write the scripts, and narrate the films, which were shot to capture not only the art itself but also the experience of attending an exhibition, including settings, lighting, and crowds. Rowland, Peach, and others on Rowland's staff photographed the shows. The foundation produced a range of documentaries, including the Paul Klee retrospective exhibition at the Guggenheim Museum in 1967, the Jackson Pollock retrospective at MoMA the same year, *The Great Age of Fresco* at the Metropolitan Museum in 1968, and *Vincent Van Gogh Paintings and Drawings*, at the Brooklyn Museum in 1971. The films were intended to circulate to museums and educational institutions across the country and were also screened abroad by the U.S. Information Agency international exchange programs.

Reaching new markets

Rowland also traveled independently to make deals for the 40/4 Chair in potential markets that GF didn't reach, often following leads from people he met at design conferences. In 1990, he took a seventeen-stop trip around the world, starting in South America, then traveling to South Africa, Australia, Indonesia, China, Japan, India, and England. He personally worked out a license agreement for the 40/4 Chair with Indovickers in Indonesia. He also didn't hesitate to travel to protect his patents if need be. One winter, he drove to Norway from Sweden in the snow to call on the Norwegian patent office, which had rejected his claim. (He won.) He was ever curious and, wherever he went, most enjoyed visiting factories.

40/4 barstools in
white and red with
coated frames.

40/4 barstools in
white and red with
coated frames.

The 40/4 family of chairs

After HOWE took over licensing the chair, Rowland worked closely with the company
to expand the 40/4 into a family of nine different models, including the original 40/4
(known as the side chair), a 40/4 swivel chair, a 40/4 barstool, a 40/4 lounge chair, and
an all-wood 40/4. Some of his variations remain in development for future release.

David Rowland: 40/4 Chair

←

40/4 barstools with
colored frames in a
hotel and conference
center restaurant in
Denmark.

↑
The 40/4 Family of
Chairs

40/4 swivel chairs in a
conference center.

David Rowland: 40/4 Chair

Rowland designed 40/4
beam seating, ideal
for public spaces,
shown here in a
healthcare waiting room
in Belgium.

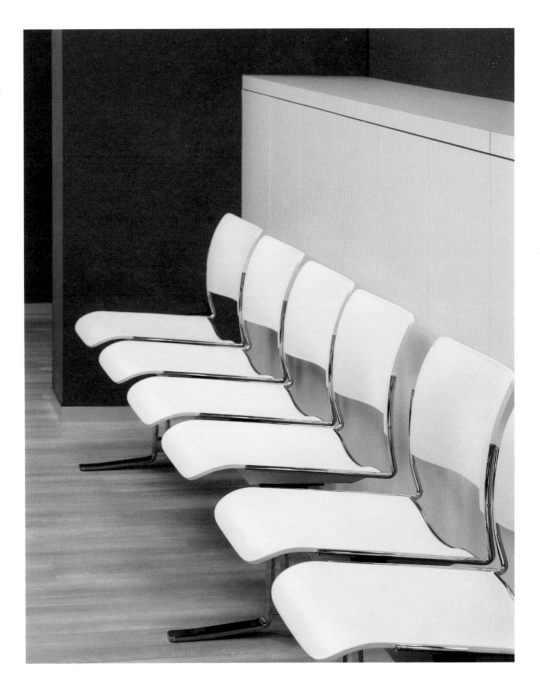

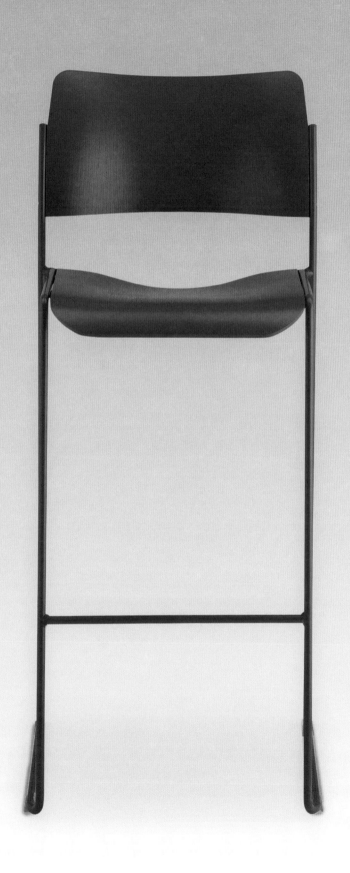

David Rowland: 40/4 Chair

Wood frame 40/4 Chairs,
in walnut and oak,
are an alternative to
the original chair with
its iconic steel rod
sled frame.

David Rowland: 40/4 Chair

Red upholstered
40/4 armchairs with
tablets and without,
UN City, Copenhagen.

Relocating to Virginia: Continuing to design

In 2001, five days before the 9/11 tragedy, Erwin and David Rowland took a trip to Marion, Virginia, because Erwin's father was having a health emergency. What was to be a short visit became a long one, as both her parents needed more help. When weeks stretched into months, they rented a house there, and Rowland worked remotely, with his assistant and secretary still at his studio on 91st Street in New York. Eventually, the Rowlands gave up their apartment in the city and sold the home in Bridgehampton, settling permanently in Virginia.

Rowland didn't miss a beat with his move to Virginia. He continued what he had always done, just from a different place. He set up a shop in the basement of his house and found local machinist and other craftspeople to help him with his experiments and to build prototypes. He was often on the phone, communicating with people everywhere. When asked how he liked his new home, he would say, "I've lived in wonderful places: California, New York, and Virginia!" Wherever his body might have been, whether it was New York or Virginia, his mind was everywhere—unconfined, never limited by place.

In addition to developing new versions of the 40/4 Chair, Rowland's last projects included a variety of other designs, such as innovative tables, new kinds of chairs, a solar-powered standing desk, and bookcases. He also focused on architecture that created homes from shipping containers. (He had for decades been interested in innovative ways to use containers for mass housing.) He also continued to see human needs in the world around him, and to design solutions to meet those needs. For example, after he witnessed devastating flooding along the Mississippi River, he developed an idea for a small-scale water-barrier system, which he patented and called Waterlog. Thinking about the need for cleaner energy, he designed a vertical-axis windmill, and was working with an engineer on an adjustable table powered by solar energy. And, of course, he continued to design chairs.

Until his passing in 2010 at age eighty-six, David Rowland continued to thrive on innovation and solving problems, "doing the most with the least." He was the definitive industrial designer, fusing the useful with beauty, leaving behind not only a masterpiece in the 40/4 Chair, but also a legacy and way of thinking that remain relevant and important today.

Design Philosophy:
A Purposeful Approach
for a Better World

A sketch of the
40/4 chair on a
placemat, 1950s.

If David Rowland's design philosophy were to be summed up in a single word, it would be "purposeful." The term can, of course, mean many things for many people. But for Rowland, to be purposeful meant designing constructive, useful products that filled a need or solved a problem, rather than products designed for the pursuit of money or style. He didn't object to profit or style as an outcome, but fulfilling a need was his North Star, his starting point, his goal, and his end result. If an object achieved its purpose with simplicity and innovation, he felt, beauty would follow.

Rowland was adamant that purposeful design could not only improve the products of daily life, but also solve the world's major problems. He pointed to the billions of people on the planet who are in need of housing, food, education, and transportation, and called upon designers to fulfill those needs as quickly as possible. He saw purposeful design as a moral choice and believed that designers have a social responsibility to create a better and more beautiful world for the benefit of all: "The service of design to the world is to be purposeful and problem-solving."

The lessons he absorbed at age sixteen studying under László Moholy-Nagy—doing the most with the least, dedication to function and simplicity, the importance of experimenting with materials, and the freedom to be visionary—permeated Rowland's career and thinking. He also knew and admired Walter Gropius, who had founded the original Bauhaus School in Germany, based on ideals that design could be an agent of positive social change. But even if Rowland hadn't studied under Moholy, no doubt the Bauhaus influence would have caught up with him as he pursued a career in industrial design. Bauhaus ideas were everywhere in the mid-century, as the greatest designers and educators grappled with the rise of industrialism, trying to reconcile beauty and art with a mass-produced world.

To be clear, Bauhaus principles contributed to Rowland's foundations, his worldview, and his skills, but he fused these ideas with his distinctive perspective and experiences to form an approach that was uniquely his own. He was individualistic, independent, and persistent in ways that went far beyond the norm. His war experiences as a bomber pilot, his family history in the American West, and his upbringing as a Christian Scientist also shaped his approach to design and the qualities of thought he brought to the process.

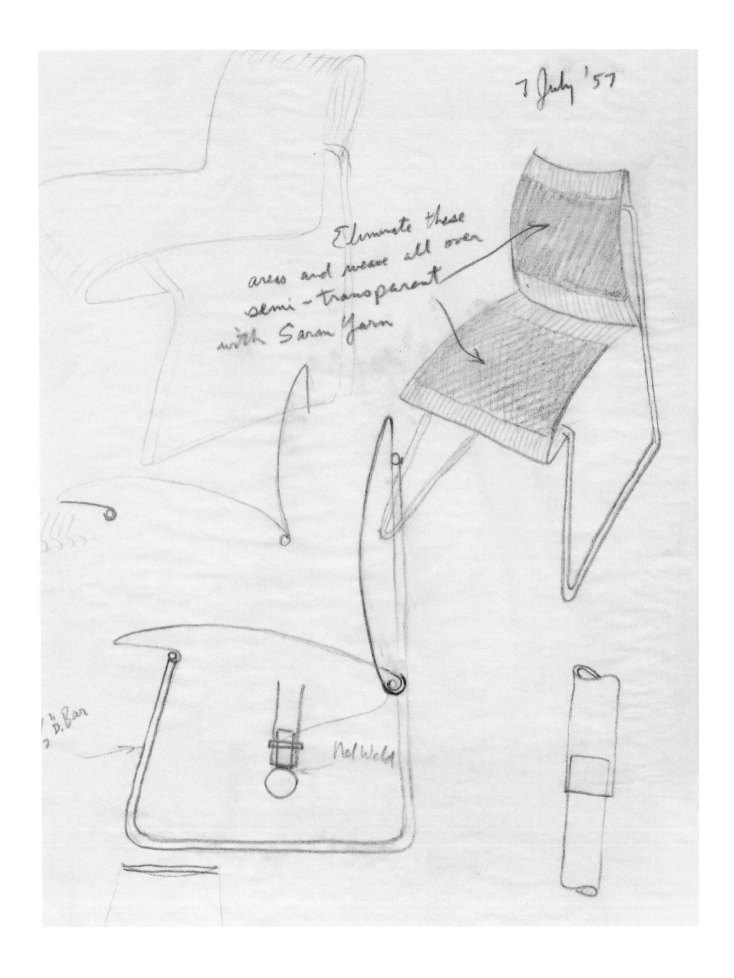

7 July '57

Eliminate these
areas and weave all over
semi-transparent
with Saran Yarn

Nol Weld

D. Bar

Rowland was constantly
working and inventing
new chair designs,
exploring multitudinous
ways of making frames,
seats, backs, and
overall structure.
Here, he calls for
semi-transparent yarn
on the seat and back.

Rowland's principles for design: A progression of thought

Rowland once described his design philosophy as a "disciplined way of thinking" based on the "election and use of parameters." He compared these parameters to the eighty-eight keys faced by a pianist, a system of limitation but also one that allows "virtually infinite" possibilities of expression.

In his speeches, writings, and conversations over forty years, Rowland distilled these parameters into a collection of important principles for purposeful design. They reflect habits of the mind and practices he cultivated faithfully. We present them here in a sequence that reflects his *progression of thought* when designing, from starting point to final product. Later in the chapter, we'll come upon Rowland's *qualities of thought*. These are the distinctive attitudes and worldview that made him successful and made the 40/4 Chair an iconic design and a masterpiece.

It's interesting to consider that, since the middle of the last century, industrial design and mass production have indeed delivered a higher standard of living around the world, as Rowland and so many of his contemporaries hoped. More people are housed, clothed, fed, and educated. And yet, as technology continues to transform the world, unmeaningful goods and services pour into our lives ever more rapidly. We now face new conflicts and needs arising from advanced technology. The importance of purposeful design is as urgent as ever.

Begin with the right motive: Beauty will follow

According to Rowland, motive is the starting point for all human-made objects and places. He was critical of designs motivated by a desire to impress. He especially criticized great monuments of history that were built for glory and of no benefit to humanity, such as the Taj Mahal, which an emperor had built in tribute to a wife who, ironically, had dedicated her life to the poor. Rowland once calculated the billions of human hours that went into creating this exotic piece of architecture filled with jewels and intricately carved gold, while so many people of India starved. He felt the same way about the great pyramids in Egypt, which cost the lives of 100,000 workers. And he liked to describe a trip to Versailles, France, where he had walked through the gilded halls in search of something useful but could not find it until he went out to a stable and picked up a strong piece of wooden floor tile.

Rowland felt similarly about the products of his own time. He questioned the value of contemporary homes designed for the purpose of beauty, but beyond the reach of most people. He asked if buildings of the "so-called established culture were really beautiful if they were much larger than any one family could afford and designed to be admired based on size and wasteful ornamentation."

Rowland also turned a critical eye on the products that flooded the market in the postwar period of growing technological power, when American factories were pumping out consumer goods. In one of his speeches, he said that all too much of the human-made world was an "ugly, inefficient, and depressing shambles." He described the experience of riding up an escalator in a department store and looking out at the bounty of goods, observing how few were "really meaningfully necessary," while outside the store he saw the threat of pollution in the ocean and air. If our "original motives were more devoted to constructive purposes," he said, "... that wouldn't happen."

Rowland frequently turned to the natural world as a guide for the right design motives because, as he explained it, nature is driven by purpose and is almost always beautiful. In a speech at the Smithsonian Institution in 1968, he asked the audience of 3,000 people to consider the oak tree, which achieves beauty because its design perfectly pursues its original purpose:

> Here is an oak tree. It came from an acorn whose sole purpose was to propagate the best tree it knew how. As it broke ground and pushed its way into the air, it had to withstand great vicissitudes. There was wind and rain, hot sun, and heavy snow loads to carry as it urged its way into space. It finally succeeded and stands as a beautiful structure, a marvelous piece of engineering, a totally purposeful shape.

When seeing the golden leaves on the sidewalk that had fallen from the ginkgo trees outside of Tiffany's jewelry store, Rowland said, "These leaves are more beautiful than anything sold inside." It was an idealized statement, and it must be added that he bought Erwin's gold wedding band from that store. But all this is not to say that Rowland called for dry utilitarian design. Quite the contrary. He loved art, and he appreciated the beauty of many human-made things. But good motives and purposeful design were always paramount for him. He deeply admired the nineteenth-century designer Michael Thonet, who embarked on an eighteen-year search for a better way to design chairs to be strong, portable, and affordable to the masses. Thonet conducted countless experiments on bending wood for mass production, a new technique at the time. This relentless persistence led to the culmination of his dream. Bent wood solved intrinsic problems in traditional chair design, namely the weakness of joints, while also providing strength and grace at an affordable price. Thonet's No. 14 chair was introduced in 1859 and is said to have sold fifty million units by 1930, and millions more ever since. It was the quintessential example of industrial design that adds value to an existing product and fulfills a practical need. The No. 14 is inexpensive and accessible to the masses through industrial production, while also bringing beauty to everyday life.

Rowland also admired the motives and beauty of simple and purposeful products, designed by people for themselves and their neighbors. His grandfather's extraordinary collection of tools created by the Indigenous People of North America stayed in his memory and imagination all his life. Rowland also admired the Shakers, who produced furniture without frivolity or fancy detailed carvings. Their simple works and their belief that "That which has in itself the highest use possesses the greatest beauty" aligned with his own values.

Designers should fill a need

"It is very much the responsibility of the designer to think out what is needed. His designing should begin with the need to be filled, and then go on to find a way to fill it better."

If the motive of good design is to be purposeful, the first step in the active design process is to identify what is needed, study why it is needed, and consider the benefits to the user.

For his 40/4 Chair, Rowland observed a need in a very personal way. As we have seen, during his bombing missions in World War II he experienced the physical pain of sitting in a bad seat. But the next part of the experience is also indicative of his process, and that was the research part. Because the missions were long, he had a lot of time to analyze the seats and think about what was needed to make them better. Observing and thinking were always key to his work and success. Later, as he began studying and designing chairs, he learned that most did not meet the needs of the human body in terms of dimensions, slope of the seat, and support. As he went deeper, he saw a need for chairs that were not only comfortable but also compact, portable, and stackable, and it was this insight that ultimately led to his great success. To live or work with Rowland was to witness him constantly looking at the world, and studying it, to improve existing conditions or find solutions to everyday problems.

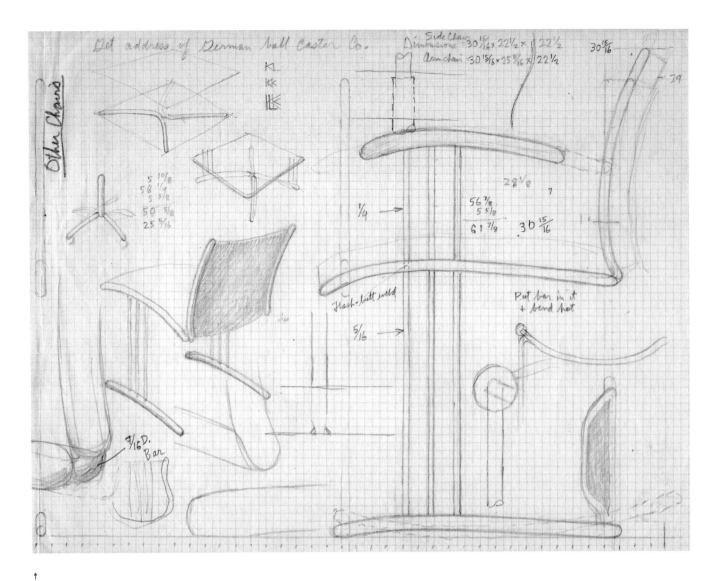

↑
Drawings, "Other
Chairs," late 1950s.
Experimental designs
for chair frames.

→
"The Dream Seat: Soft
as a Dream." Early
on, Rowland wanted
his chairs to deliver
comfort without bulky
padding. This led
him to invent new
materials that were
supportive while, at
the same time, soft and
comfortable. As this
sketch notes, he also
designed chairs with
removable upholstery
for easy cleaning or
change of look.

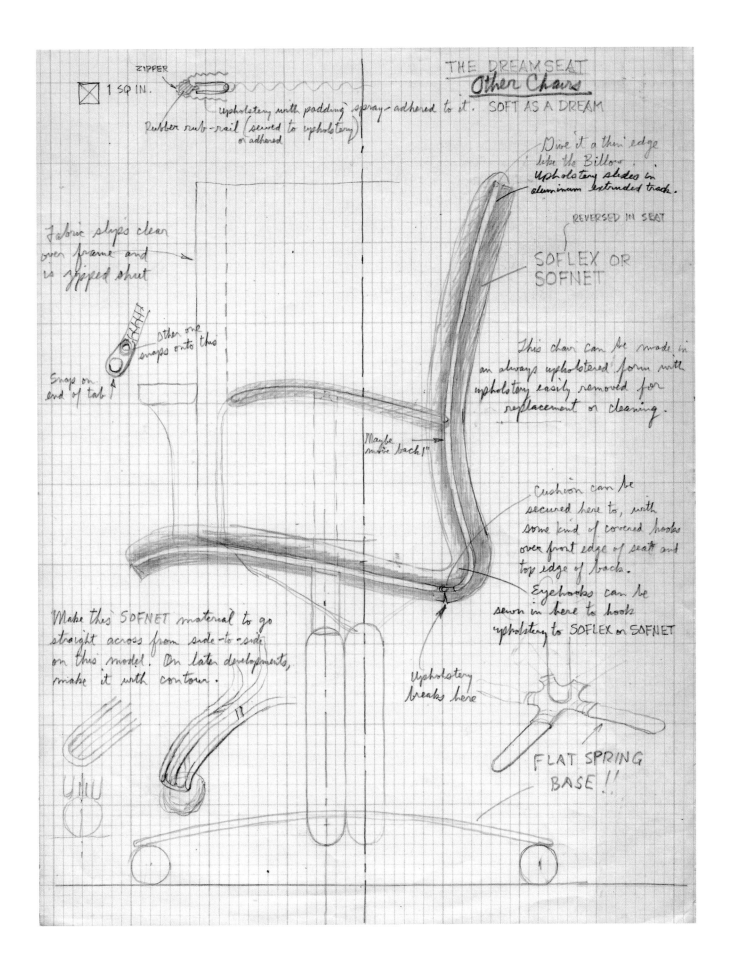

ZIPPER

☒ 1 SQ IN.

upholstery with padding spray-adhered to it.

Rubber rub-rail (sewed to upholstery or adhered)

Give it a thin edge like the Billow. Upholstery slides in aluminum extruded track.

REVERSED IN SEAT

SOFLEX OR SOFNET

Fabric slips clear over frame and is zipped shut

Other one snaps onto this

Snap on end of tab

This chair can be made in an always "upholstered" form with upholstery easily removed for replacement or cleaning.

Maybe move back 1"

Cushion can be secured here to, with some kind of covered hooks over front edge of seat and top edge of back.

Eyehooks can be sewn in here to hook upholstery to SOFLEX or SOFNET

Make this SOFNET material to go straight across from side-to-side on this model. On later developments, make it with contour.

Upholstery breaks here

FLAT SPRING BASE !!

Rowland's imagination was
ever-active, exploring
chair design ideas.

David Rowland: 40/4 Chair

Listen to the Divine Mind

Once a need is identified, it is time to come up with design ideas that will meet that need. Where would these ideas come from? Rowland believed that his ideas didn't come from inside of himself, but from a spiritual source outside. Raised as a Christian Scientist from birth, he understood God to be the ultimate creator, the all-good and all-knowing Divine Mind. When he was designing, he listened to the Divine Mind for ideas. What did this mean? For Rowland, to listen to God was to be open and receptive to the voice that speaks to us all the time through ideas and intuitions. In 1954, he was listening to the Divine Mind when the idea for his 40/4 Chair came to him. He was listening when all his other design ideas came to him as well. The Divine Mind not only offered new ideas but helped Rowland solve problems. Once, when he was on the factory floor of a company that was making parts for his Soflex material, a manufacturing problem arose that seemed unsolvable. At that moment Rowland paused to listen for guidance. The thought came to him "Tell the men to slow down the machines." He did so, and immediately the parts began to come out perfectly.

There were no limits to creative ideas because there were no limits to God. There were always good ideas to be found. Gratitude also played a major role in being receptive to God. Rowland saw gratitude as a choice, a mental habit that could be learned and strengthened. It was his daily practice and a key element of his resilience when he hit low moments of disinterest and rejection. This optimistic view of the universe and capacity for gratitude were a profound source of strength that fueled Rowland's life, creative career, and the products he designed, from beginning to end.

Design should express its materials

Rowland was constantly experimenting with materials, going back to his time at Cranbrook. He spent decades experimenting with the capacities of seating built with wire, plastics, steel tubing, and especially sinuous metal springs, which appear in so many of his designs. He loved the strength and give of springs, which create the comfort of an upholstered chair without the bulky padding. As a result of these experiments, he invented Soflex, an entirely new material that broke boundaries and allowed him to invent chairs that had never been made before. Today, Rowland would tell designers to look to the many new high-tech materials that are arriving and to experiment with them, pushing the boundaries of their possibilities and applications.

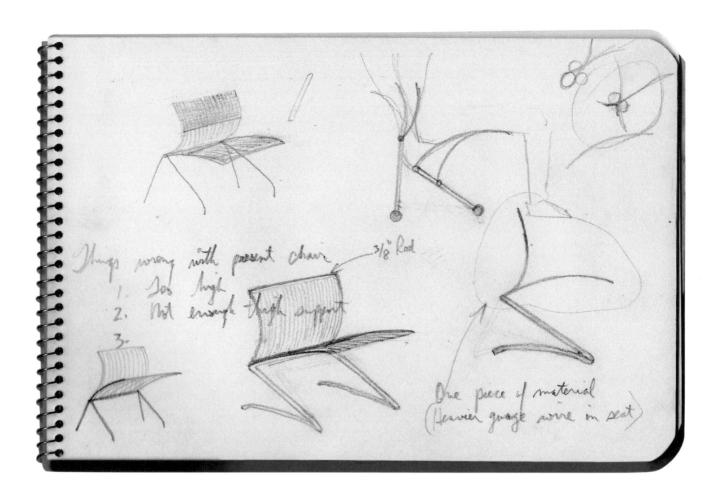

Sketch with a self-
critique of his
designs: "Too high…not
enough thigh support."

A barrel-style chair
with a scallop finish
made of "corrugate like
seashell," 1950s.

Rowland initially
designed stylish chairs
to seek Florence
Knoll's approval.
Later, he realized that
he should focus on
invention and design
a new kind of chair
with added features
and functions.

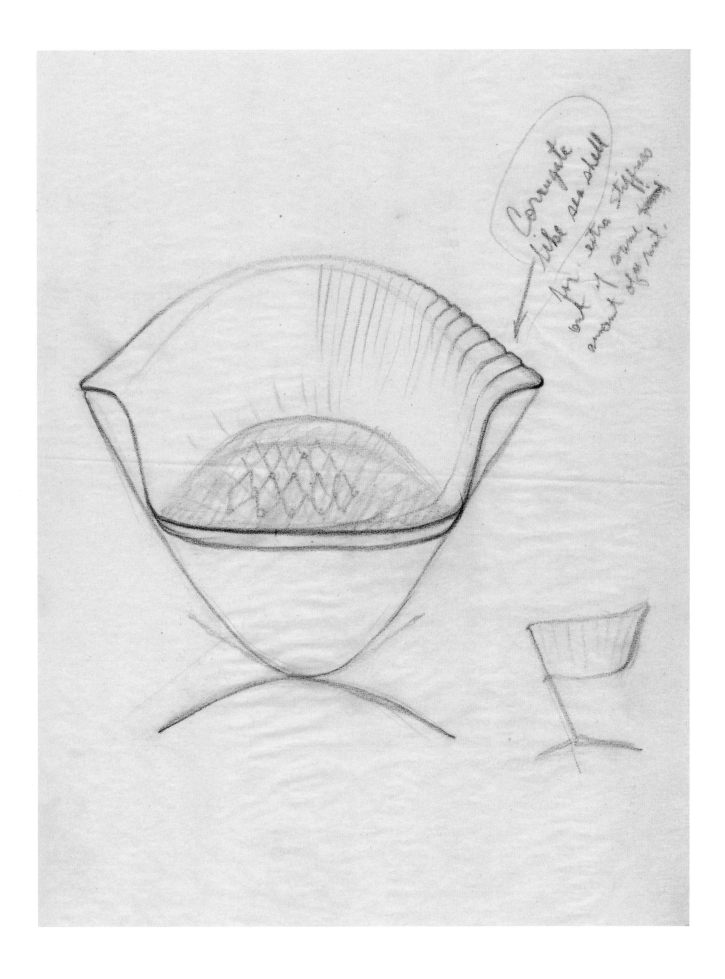

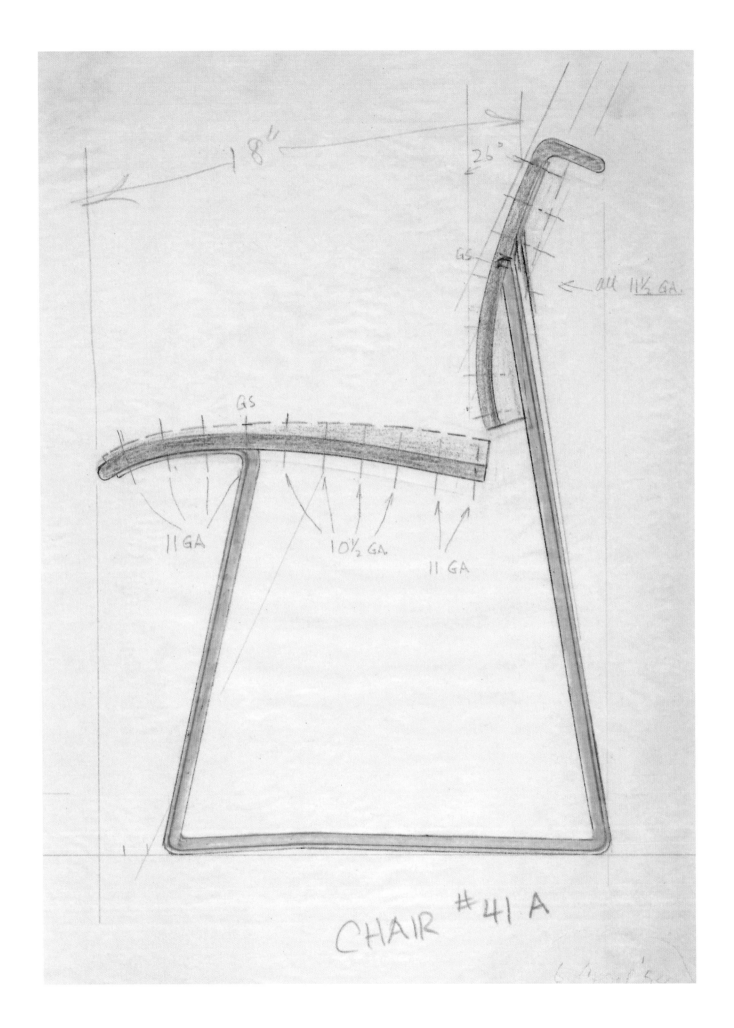

18"

26°

GS

← all 11½ GA.

GS

11 GA

10½ GA

11 GA

CHAIR #41 A

Chair 41A. Though the
seat and back are not
yet connected, the
design for the 40/4
Chair is emerging in
this drawing.

Innovate, invent, and think beyond limits

Invention was Rowland's passion, his approach to design, his process, and his result. He was a designer in his soul, but a part of him was also an engineer, who engaged deeply with how things worked—and how they could work better. Many mid-century designers, such as Raymond Loewy, focused on style and appearance. That was a fine purpose for many, but not for Rowland, whose starting point was what a product could do. He designed from the inside out, experimenting relentlessly to innovate new products that worked differently or to add new value to an existing product. He liked to say, "The different is seldom better, but the better is always different."

Rowland understood that to be an innovator requires imagination and going where others haven't gone before, regardless of negative feedback and arguments about why new things can't be done. Rowland liked to quote the English man of letters Samuel Johnson: "Nothing will ever be attempted if all possible objections must first be overcome."

Rowland believed good design is visionary. In his speeches, he often said that a designer's service to society is to see years ahead, where consumers and companies cannot. "Ten years hence there will be any number of new products we have never seen before. Where do they come from? They come from imaginative thinking which is interested in delving into the future and bringing those things into the now." This required seeing needs before the consumer and companies could see or want those needs filled. "The public influences design. So do the manufacturer and the salesman. But the designer must do the designing ... Public acceptance and sales potential are important disciplines, but they must remain an influence on design thinking, not a replacement for it."

Rowland's friend Bucky Fuller often spoke about the lag between the designer's futuristic thinking and public acceptance of breakthrough products. It takes time for consumers to catch up and embrace what is different, because it is unfamiliar. Fuller believed that the designer must embrace and plan for this lag as part of the process. Rowland, whose designs were often radically different and ahead of their time, understood this lag all too well.

Do the most with the least

Rowland removed ornamentation and excess, paring down his designs relentlessly to be as simple as possible while still achieving their ideal function. He also believed that limitations forced a designer to create a better design, and that, often, the least costly products were as good as or better than the expensive ones. Doing the most with the least allows the designer to invent products that are affordable and can reach the masses quickly and benefit humanity with efficiency and speed. Recycling or using what already exists was always on Rowland's mind and explains why he loved to visit junkyards and the bins of secondhand goods on Canal Street in New York City.

One repeating theme in Rowland's designs was the upward arch in the seat to allow "give" when sat upon. The chair circled in red suggests an early version of the Billow Chair.

Be a comprehensivist, not a specialist

Rowland was a holistic designer, concerned with the entire design process, from beginning to end: identifying and researching the need, inventing and patenting the design, locating and licensing a manufacturer, working with the manufacturer to perfect the manufacturing process, being on the factory floor, promoting the design (by giving talks to designers and architects), and thinking of improvements and refinements to later iterations. He invented machinery and materials for his chairs, as in the case of Soflex, which he used in his Softec and Billow chairs. In this he was ahead of his time. As the world has grown more complex and global, thinkers in every field have embraced cross-disciplinary thinking and collaborations for finding solutions to the world's biggest problems.

David Rowland: 40/4 Chair

Early 1950s chair
experiments, including
many kinds of bases and
a hammock-style seat.

Make your own opportunities

When Rowland began his career, he arrived in New York without connections or money. The independent path he took required faith in himself and hard work, which had been instilled in him by his family. Over time, he developed a formula for success: to identify a need, listen for ideas, experiment with materials, innovate and invent a product, patent the product, then license it for manufacture. He did all these steps largely on his own, as an independent entity without a company to underwrite costs. In life and business, he had no hesitation to reach out to people and put himself in front of influencers, introducing himself and his latest ideas.

Patenting his ideas was extremely important to Rowland. It allowed him to earn royalties and keep his independence financially, so that he could continue to design on his own terms. He put great thought and care into writing his patents, which were mostly utility patents and therefore stronger than design patents.

When Rowland spoke to industrial designers, he encouraged them to "build a better mousetrap" in their home workshops and to protect their winning inventions by getting patents. For those who were employed by a company and forced to sign away patent rights for developments in the employer's field, he encouraged them to negotiate an agreement that allowed them to pursue inventions in other areas. He believed passionately that the market would reward great ideas.

In the drawing: 11 May '55 — Tapered Legs — For Resilient Ribbon

↑

In the upper right, a
sketch of a chair with
a sled base suggests
the 40/4 design to
come, 1955.

→

Straight lines and
curves. An early chair
idea that combined a
dramatic cantilever
base and an elegantly
curved seat and back.
This is the side view
of the drawing on
page 223.

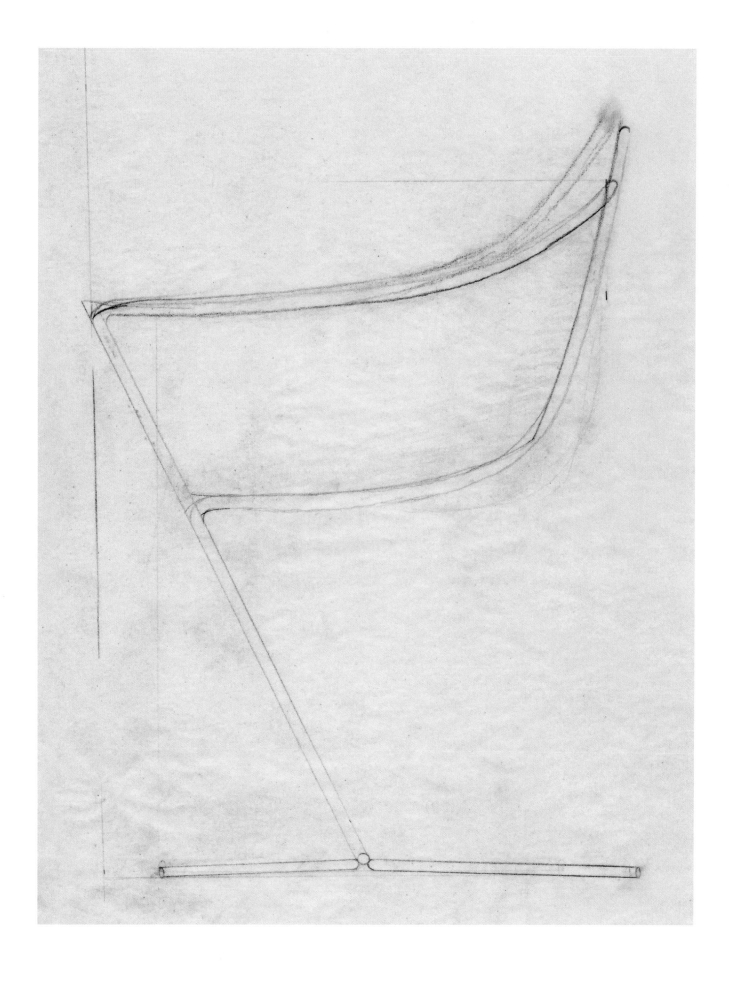

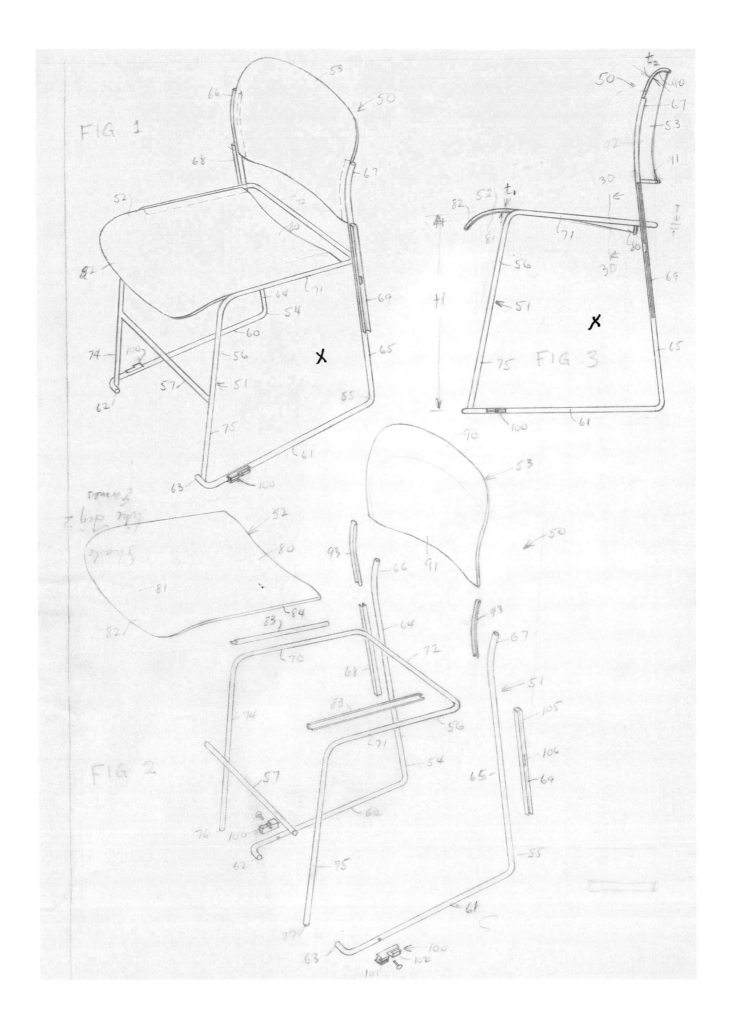

David Rowland: 40/4 Chair

Rowland's technical
drawing with detailed
specifications for
the 40/4.

Always bounce back. Never give up

Rowland's nine-year effort to bring the 40/4 Chair to market is a case study in persistence, but also a critical part of his legacy, arguably as much as his masterpiece chair itself. He understood that innovation required not only imagination, but also a willingness to fail and a fearlessness to do so. His religious conviction that he was not alone in the world no doubt contributed to his courage. But his persistence was ultimately founded on his self-reliance and work ethic. He went back to the drawing board time and again, not only trying harder, but also thinking more deeply about design problems and solutions. He bounced back repeatedly in his efforts to find a manufacturer. When he finally got his licensing deal with General Fireproofing, it was bigger than he could have imagined, and success was immediate. When Rowland encountered difficulties, he remembered his motto: "ABB," which stood for "Always Bounce Back."

One person can make a difference

Rowland loved to inspire other designers and thinkers. And he loved the idea that the work we do may never be finished but continued by others. This quotation from Walter Gropius was taped above Rowland's drafting table:

> Act as if you were going to live forever and cast your plans way ahead. By this I mean that you must feel responsible without time and limitation, and the consideration whether you may or may not be around to see the results should never enter your thoughts. If your contribution has been vital, there will always be somebody to pick up where you left off, and that will be your claim to immortality.

Purpose was a path for design, but it was also a path for living. Rowland believed that we all have an individual purpose for being alive, and that to achieve it we must be ourselves and follow our own path. When we pursue our purpose, a single human being can have a positive impact on the world.

Index

Select bibliography

Much of the material for this book came from unpublished sources, including David's writings about his life and career, letters, and family archival material, interviews with his staff, 40/4 promotional material from GF, David's speeches on industrial design, and my memories from forty years of marriage. In addition, the following sources were used.

ER

Books, periodicals, websites

Bacchi, Anna and Giorgio. "13th Milan Triennale." *Arts & Architecture* 81, no. 12, December 1964.

Eckardt, Wolf von. "Smithsonian Exhibit of Chairs Reveals the Measure of Man." *The Washington Post*, December 22, 1968.

Eddy, Mary Baker. *Science and Health with Key to the Scriptures*, 1875.

Emery, Sherman R. "To Fill a Need." *Interior Design*, February 1965.

Fiell, Charlotte and Peter. *1000 Chairs*. Cologne: Taschen, 1997.

Hevesi, Dennis. "David Rowland, 86, Maker of a Tidily Stacked Chair." *The New York Times*, August 26, 2010.

Interiors. "David Rowland's 40/4 Chair." June 1964.

Kamin, Blair. "A Small Show about Chairs Hints at Larger Design Ambitions at the Art Institute." *Chicago Tribune*, August 26, 2016.

Kane, Patricia E. *300 Years of American Seating Furniture: Chairs and Beds from the Mabel Brady Garvan and Other Collections at Yale University*. Boston: New York Graphic Society, 1976.

Keller, Hadley. "11 Product Designs So Ubiquitous We Forget About Them." *Architectural Digest*, July 25, 2017.

Meadmore, Clement. *The Modern Chair: Classics in Production*. New York: Van Nostrand Reinhold Company, 1975.

Moholy-Nagy, László, *Vision in Motion*. Paul Theobald & Co., 1947.

The New York Times. "U.S. Exhibit Takes Top Prize in Milan." September 26, 1964.

Pictorial Living. "Top Designs for '65." January 17, 1965. *Product Engineering*. "Master Designs of 1964." May 10, 1965.

Product Engineering. "Rowland Talks Design and Wire." November 22, 1965.

Richardson, Lucy Ryder. *100 Midcentury Chairs: and their stories*. Gibbs Smith, 2017.

Robinson, Von. "99% Perspiration." *Metropolis Magazine*, December 2004.

Rowland, David. "Stackable Chair: Designer David Rowland Tells How at First, Everyone Turned It Down..." *The Christian Science Monitor*. October 6, 1988.

Rybczynski, Witold. *Now I Sit Me Down: From Klismos to Plastic Chair: A Natural History*. New York: Ferrar, Straus and Giroux, 2016.

Schwartz, Marvin D. *Please Be Seated: The Evolution of the Chair*. [Exhibition Catalog.] The American Federation of Arts, 1968.

Sieden, Steven L. *A Fuller View: Buckminster Fuller's Vision of Hope and Abundance for All*. Divine Arts Press, 2012.

Sisson, Patrick. "The New Bauhaus, a radical design school before its time," https://archive.curbed.com, 2019

University Library | University of Illinois Chicago, "Circle First to Use 40/4 Chairs," https://library.uic.edu/, 2015.

Biographical information on midcentury designers

Buckminster Fuller: https://www.bfi.org/about-fuller/big-ideas/livingry/

Florence Knoll: "Remembering the Remarkable Florence Knoll, Modern Design Pioneer." https://www.pbs.org/wgbh/roadshow/stories/articles/2019/1/28/remembering-remarkable-florence-knoll, February 2019.

Edgar Kaufmann Jr.: https://www.moma.org/interactives/exhibitions/2016/spelunker/constituents/2486/

László Moholy-Nagy: https://www.moholy-nagy.org

Maria Bergson: https://interiordesign.net/designwire/maria-bergson/

Norman Bel Geddes: https://www.idsa.org/profile/norman-bel-geddes/

Raymond Lowey: https://www.raymondloewy.org/loewy-biography/

Picture credits

Photograph by Claude K. Allen: 151; Photograph by Javier Azurmendi: 148; Courtesy of California Art Club: 36 (b); Photograph by Ole Christiansen: 154–155; Image owned by Commercial Furniture Group, Inc., and used by Howe a/s. Used with permission. All rights reserved: 14, 25, 26–27, 140, 173, 180; Image owned by Commercial Furniture Group, Inc. and used with permission: 182–183, 184, 185, 187, 190–191; Photograph by Richard G. Askew. Courtesy Cranbrook Archives: 65; © Lara Swimmer/Esto: 152–153; Photograph by Angel Gil: 156–157; Photograph by Toon Grobet: 203; Image owned by Howe a/s, Used with permission. All rights reserved: 24, 141, 149, 172, 201, 204, 205; Photograph by Niall Clutton. Image owned by Howe a/s. Used with permission. All rights reserved: 142; Photograph by Stuart McIntyre. Image owned by Howe a/s. Used with permission. All rights reserved: 144, 199; Photograph by Skovdal Nordic. Image owned by Howe a/s. Used with permission. All rights reserved: 200, 202, 206, 207; Photograph by Dieter Leistner: 160–161; © 2023 Estate of László Moholy-Nagy / Artists Rights Society (ARS), New York: 40 (r); Photograph by James Morris: 162–163; Photograph by Efrain Pinto: 158; © 2023 The Pollock-Krasner Foundation / Artists Rights Society (ARS), New York: 198; The Principia Archives, Principia College, Elsah, Illinois: 54; Courtesy of Erwin Rowland and the David Rowland Estate: 10, 16, 18, 20, 21, 22, 23, 30, 32 (t), 32 (b), 35, 36 (t), 40 (l), 42 (l), 42 (r), 43, 44, 45, 46, 50, 52, 53, 55, 56 (t), 56 (b), 57 (t), 57 (b), 58, 59 (t), 59 (b), 60, 61, 62 (t), 62 (b), 63, 64 (t), 64 (b), 66, 67, 69, 70, 74, 76, 77 (t), 77 (b), 80, 81, 82, 83 (t), 83 (b), 92, 93, 94, 95 (t), 95 (b), 96, 97, 98 (t), 98 (b), 100, 101, 106, 110, 111, 114, 116 (t), 116 (b), 117 (t), 117 (b), 126, 128, 170, 174 (t), 174 (b), 175, 176, 177, 179, 192, 193 (t), 193 (b), 212, 214, 218, 219, 220, 222, 223, 224, 226, 227, 228, 230, 231, 232; Photograph courtesy of Dave Stuckey: 123; Norman Bel Geddes Theater and Industrial Design Papers, Harry Ransom Center, The University of Texas at Austin: 88, 90, 91.

Acknowledgements

My heartfelt thanks to Mitzi Vernon, former Dean of the College of Design at the University of Kentucky, who was an early champion of this project, assisted with research and opened doors. I am also grateful to Michael Jacobsen, longtime president and CEO of HOWE a/s, which manufactures the 40/4 Chair with fidelity to David's design and made many of the beautiful images in this book available. I am also grateful to HOWE's Izabela Woźniak and Anette Hagemann Ribold for their help with those images. Many thanks to Seamus Bateson, CEO of Commercial Furniture Group (CFGroup), for contributing images from GF and Thonet USA. I thank Carl Gustav Magnusson, who provided encouragement, insights, and the foreword to the book; Malcolm Peach, who worked for David for many years and gave interviews and memories; and architect Jeanne Gang, who introduced me to Phaidon. Thanks, also, to designer Candace Butler, who helped with images; Blair Linford, my technical expert; Tod Owens of Smyth-Bland Regional Library; my friend Connie Osborne, who assisted with archives; and Bo Bogatin, for his wise counsel.

I am ever grateful to Bonnie Siegler of Eight and a Half for introducing me to Arielle Eckstut of The Book Doctors, who introduced me to Laura Schenone, my collaborator, coauthor, and partner in this work. Laura helped shape the book from the initial concept to the finished product and kept the project on track time and again. I am deeply thankful for her exceptional writing and storytelling talents, expertise, dedication, patience, and guidance. Without Laura, this book would not have been possible.

Above all, my deep gratitude to Phaidon Press for bringing the book to life, with special appreciation to project editor Rosie Pickles, who brought skill and patience to countless details; Michael Bierut and Jonny Sikov at Pentagram for their elegant design; production controller Zuzana Cimalova and the rest of the Phaidon team who supported this work. Most of all, I thank Emilia Terragni, associate publisher and editorial director at Phaidon, who immediately understood and embraced the idea for this book and then gave her legendary expertise, guidance, and vision to make it a beautiful reality. I couldn't be more appreciative.

ER

Phaidon Press Limited
2 Cooperage Yard
London E15 2QR

Phaidon Press Inc.
111 Broadway
New York, NY 10006

phaidon.com

First published 2024
© 2024 Phaidon Press Limited

ISBN 978 1 83866 812 9

A CIP catalogue record for this book is available from the British Library and the Library of Congress.

Commissioning Editor
Emilia Terragni

Project Editor
Rosie Pickles

Production Controller
Zuzana Cimalova

Design
Michael Bierut and
Jonny Sikov, Pentagram

Printed in China